The Quest of the Infinite

The Quest of the Infinite

OR

The Place of Reason and Mystery in Religious Experience

By

BENJAMIN A. MILLARD

GYAN

Published by

GYAN

Gyan Publishing House
5, Ansari Road
Daryaganj, New Delhi-110002
Phone: 011-47034999, 9811692060
E-mail: books@gyanbooks.com

Distribution Network
gyanbooks.com
India, USA, Canada, UK, Australia, France

ISBN : 978-81-212-6792-2 (PB)
First Published, 1905

2nd Impression 2022

Printed at: Gyan Press, Delhi.

THE QUEST OF THE INFINITE
Author: BENJAMIN A. MILLARD

THE QUEST OF THE INFINITE

OR

The Place of Reason and Mystery in Religious Experience

By

BENJAMIN A. MILLARD

1905

CONTENTS

Contents

PREFACE

THE quest of the average man to-day is to find a simple but sufficient ground for Faith. He has no real preference for unbelief, by nature he inclines to Faith.

But he is practical, and has a feeling for reality If he makes the Christian Faith his own it must be for reasons, and reasons which are fairly simple and appeal directly to his common sense and to his own experience. The average man has really done with Authority as a ground of Faith. He has not the time, nor as a rule the training, to follow his quest along the lines of philosophy or of theology in its more scientific aspects.

Theological subtilties only perplex and worry him, and often obscure his vision.

They are not in his line, and produce in him an impression of unreality about Religion. It is upon this impression that recent campaigns of criticism have fastened and with which they have played. "Religion, Christianity is only a juggle of metaphysics, bolstered up by the chicanery of interested ministrants," it has been urged. "Come out with us into the light of common-sense."

The aim of the following papers is to show that religion is not in essence theological, however useful and necessary theology may be on its scientific side. The surest ground for Faith in Christ and participation in the good news which He brought is neither theology, nor metaphysics, nor science, but simple experience, the experience of each individual; and here the average man is quite at home. The appeal urged in what follows is simply this: give Jesus Christ the opportunity of doing His work in your own heart and life; give Him a fair chance, and then judge Him by the results.

Preface

It is along this line that the average man may most readily and effectually be influenced. This was the first method of the Christian Apologetic, and except for the scholar and theologian (and really in the final outcome for them also) it is the last. Upon the broad fact of what Jesus is to us and does for us in our own individual experience of Him, must rest our ultimate reasons for faith in Him as Saviour and Lord.

BENJAMIN A. MILLARD.

THE PLACE OF MYSTERY IN RELIGION

CHAPTER I

THE PLACE OF MYSTERY IN RELIGION

IT is frequently urged against Religion that it is so full of mystery, it makes so large a demand for faith.

In an age that is essentially curious, that craves for absolute certainty, and is impatient to analyse everything down to its simplest elements, to leave nothing unresolved, no question unanswered, the value of Religion is tested by the standard of obviousness. The demand of the age is for a Religion which makes everything quite plain and easy, and, leaving no region of life or thought unexplored, has no reserve, no mystery. It would seem as though the first essential for the discussion of Religion were that we should refuse to recognize in it any legitimate place for the element of the mysterious. Faith is held in contempt, and is caricatured as the capacity for believing the unbelievable.

"If Religion is to be satisfactory," it is said, "it must leave nothing unexplained, it must answer all questions. If you expect us to believe in God, you must define Him with logical accuracy and completeness, and analyse the constituents of His Being as the chemist analyses the constituents of water. If you expect us to believe in the goodness of God and in the operation of a benevolent Providence, you must furnish us with an entirely flawless explanation of all the facts which seem to contradict it, an explanation which shall leave no loophole for any apparent exception to creep through its ring-fence of logic. You must perfectly reconcile the two opposite sets of facts, one set of which points to man's freedom, and the other to his limitations. You must furnish us with a complete analysis of man's nature, and a clue to its complexities, you must give us a demonstrable account of his origin and a verifiable statement of his destiny. You must tell us what happens to man after his death; and if you expect us to believe in the reality of anything beyond the seen and material you must show it to us, just as you can take us into the next street and show us its houses and the people in them. When you can bring us a Religion that does all this, then we will accept it."

Is it not the failure of Religion to answer those questions, to resolve all mystery, to clear away the haze of uncertainty that hangs about the horizon of life and thought, which lies at the root of much of the popular impatience with Religion? It has been tried in this respect and found wanting, and therefore is cast aside with scarcely veiled contempt.

And it is not the critics of Religion alone who are responsible for this misconception. The Christian Church, teachers of Religion, theologians, often take up an attitude which suggests that they are quite willing and able to respond to the challenge of their critics and provide a creed, a system of theology which shall settle absolutely all questions, shall leave no room for doubt, or a suspended judgment ; shall indeed make doubt intellectually impossible, and morally sinful ; allowing no place for two opinions on any matter, removing every element of mystery, make it so that only the fool or the wicked man shall hesitate to accept the theology or the creed. So people to-day are pathetically asking : "Is this then a true account of what Religion ought to do ? Does Religion involve absolute certainty on all things that come within its scope ? If my Religion still leaves wide regions where in humble reverence I have to walk by faith and not by sight ; if God is still far above and beyond me past finding out, unmeasurable ; if there remain many problems about which I have to confess that I cannot finally solve them, am I to give up my Religion as a delusion, a mere leap in the dark that can bring no real help, no abiding comfort ? "

Now let us acknowledge, frankly and fearlessly, that Religion, so far from abolishing mystery, is itself, and must ever be, full of the element of the mysterious and unresolved. Even our Christian Religion leaves many questions unanswered ; questions, too, which we think demand an answer, urgent questions which arise out of our better nature and its deepest longings, its holiest aspirations, and are not merely the product of an impatient and shallow curiosity. Indeed, it may be said that Christianity brings into Religion certain elements which tend to deepen the mystery.

One of the great messages of Religion to man is to justify the presence of mystery, to proclaim that in the very nature of things it is inevitable, that there must ever remain some questions which cannot be answered. A dogmatism that leaves no room for doubt, that excommunicates a different opinion, that removes the necessity for faith, is essentially irreligious.

Having made this acknowledgment, how are we to justify it? We accept the criticism of Religion as inevitable, how are we to defend it? How can we recommend as rational and necessary a Religion of mystery?

To begin with, it may be observed that, with a strange and suggestive inconsistency, the critics who demand that any Religion which they can accept must be clear and absolute in all its answers, must leave no room for hesitancy, are the very first to cry out against anything that sounds like a note of certainty in the voice of Religion, and sneer at what they call the "dogmatism" of theology, its pretension to "infallibility."

What is this but the instinctive protest of the mind against the very thing which they demand?

As soon as they are offered anything approaching the absolute answers for which they ask, their deeper consciousness awakens to its incongruity.

But let us pass that by and go on to seek some positive justification for the element of mystery in Religion. And we may well ask, could it be otherwise? Is it not exactly what one ought to expect? Would any Religion that had no mystery in it be worth our accepting? Would it not be a contradiction in terms?

The first test of the value of Religion is that it should be true to the facts of life; it must accept them as they are, and not try to explain them away. What we find in life should have its complement in Religion.

For example: we find in life the fact of the supremacy of law, the principles of sacrifice, of progress, of development. Any Religion which denies or ignores these is sure to be unsatisfactory, to break down in contradictions and ineffectiveness.

Now life is full of mystery, from beginning to end, in its greatest things and in its smallest.

Take the simplest flower that grows in our garden: a question or two about it from the little child beside us brings us to the confines of a wonderland of mystery in which we too become as a child. Or the radiant fact of the mother's love in which the little one has lived and grown into loveliness of soul brings us into the presence of a tender mystery, a mystery more marvellous than that which lies in the flower's life.

There is not one of the many experiences of the daily life which, however commonplace and understandable it seems, has not close behind it a whole world of inexplicable mystery. We cannot swerve a hair's breadth from the narrow track of the ordinary without plunging into mystery; indeed, that narrow track itself grows mysterious as soon as we begin to consider it closely. The ordinary is only the mysterious grown familiar and taken for granted; our explanations of its phenomena only lead to other questions which we cannot answer.

And is Religion to ignore this mystery which confronts us on every hand in life? We find deep-rooted in life what we may call an element of "hiddenness"—a principle of reserve. All our knowledge, all the daily revelations of science and every new perception of the relations of things make it more and more abundantly plain that the increase of knowledge widens the horizon of the unknown. Every explanation of a fact brings into view other facts that await still further explanation. One of the things which the wonderful growth of knowledge in recent times declares with the greatest emphasis is, that there is a certain inexhaustibleness in the world and in human life. However far we travel along the path of the known, the unknown must still stretch beyond us. The greater our knowledge, the closer and more accurate our acquaintance with the phenomena of life, the wider and deeper grows the mystery.

Is Religion to violate this principle of

hiddenness, to deny the fact of the inexhaustibleness of things, to set itself in opposition to the reality of mystery? Then it would be untrue to life, it would contradict our knowledge of life, it would stand self-condemned.

The fact that Religion recognizes and accepts the ultimate mystery of things is one of its great justifications. It at any rate corresponds to what we find in life. The man who recognizes his own limitations will be the readiest to agree that Religion also, to be true and real, must recognize that same principle of limitations; which is only another way of saying that Religion must have its element of mystery.

Not only is the element of mystery justified of its place in Religion by its corresponding place in life, but it plays a very large part in the origin of Religion. Religion is, in one way, the direct outcome of the mystery in life.

Wordsworth describes the quickening of the higher nature, the birth of the soul, as happening just at the moment when the mystery of nature and of life is recognized as a fundamental fact, as a happy reality, and not as a curse to be resented—

> . . . that blessed mood,
> In which the burthen of the mystery,
> In which the heavy and the weary weight
> Of all this unintelligible world,
> Is lightened.

Religion is the response of the soul to the fact of the mystery in life, it arises out of the recognition of the element of the mysterious, and its progress is the growth and fulfilment of the soul under the influence of union and fellowship with the great mystery which lies enshrined in life, and penetrates to and haunts its every phase and detail.

Look at Religion in its crudest and most primitive manifestations. All that lies outside the obvious, all things that are beyond the narrow limits of the savage man's understanding, form the groundwork, the starting point of his Religion.

Or consider the same experience as expressed in the thought and life of the most cultured and learned and resolute of thinkers, whose store of knowledge seems to the average man almost inexhaustible. There is not one of them but has to acknowledge that he arrives at a point somewhere beyond which there is nothing but mystery, where the only answer to the questions which still crowd upon him is—"I do not know," a point where faith has to take the place of knowledge, where the seen melts into the unseen, where the soul is only conscious of

> A presence that disturbs me with the joy
> Of elevated thoughts: a sense sublime
> Of something far more deeply interfused,
> Whose dwelling is the light of setting suns,
> And the round ocean and the living air,
> And the blue sky, and in the mind of man:
> A motion and a spirit, that impels
> All thinking things, all objects of all thought,
> And rolls through all things.

And that "something," that "motion" and "spirit" which "rolls through all things," to the acknowledgment of which the search for knowledge ultimately brings us, is the root fact of Religion ; out of it grow the fair flowers of faith and love and hope, of purity and goodness and truth, in communion with which the soul finds the adequate sphere for its own fulfilment.

The element of mystery, then, has a legitimate and inevitable place in Religion, just as, and indeed because, it has an undeniable place in life. The consciousness of its presence awakens the soul ; it is the quickening impulse in the life of the soul and affords the fitting scope for the soul's fulfilment. Unconsciousness of its reality, or a refusal to recognize its place and its function, results in a Religion without power, and a nature stunted and starved by a lack of correspondence with its environment. A Religion which ignores or denies the necessary mystery as an ultimate fact in its outlook on life is its own refutation, for in that deficiency it removes its own *raison d'être*.

There now remains the question, what is

the active relation of Religion to the element of mystery, how does Religion interpret the mystery of life ? Religion accepts the fact, what explanation does it offer of its presence ?

The fact must be dealt with in some way, its presence has some significance, some explanation must be offered for it. What does a material philosophy offer in the way of explanation ?

Nothing. It has perforce to recognize its presence, and there it leaves it. Scientific materialism has some time to come to the "I do not know, I cannot tell," as the final point of inquiry ; but it has no suggestion to make as to the significance of its own limitations. Its vaunted certainty in all things only leads it to a region of uncertainty, and there its mission ends. It has no further word to say, it does not attempt to interpret the root-fact of the mystery of life.

But what is the interpretation which Religion offers ?

The attitude of Religion to the mystery of

life may be briefly summed up as follows :—

1. Religion recognizes the fact as inevitable. It frankly acknowledges that there must be many things which are beyond our finding out That there is and ever must be an unknown land fronting the soul however far it travels along the path of experience and knowledge. The horizon of the soul is illimitable.

2. Then Religion goes on to tell us why this is so. It tells us that there is a mystery in life, because life is more than material—it is spiritual. The presence of mystery is the emergence into the material of the spiritual, and the penetration of the material by the spiritual. The element of the mysterious is the element of the spiritual manifesting itself in the realm of the material. The world and human life are mysterious because they are the concrete expression, and of necessity the partial expression, of a spiritual *Reality* that lies behind them. That spiritual Reality it calls God. The mystery in life is God manifesting Himself—it is His thought, His pur-

pose, His activity expressed in terms of human thought and experience; it is the veiled God standing before us.

And God is inexhaustible, unmeasurable, illimitable, and past our finding out. You cannot get rid of mystery from life or from Religion until you can abolish God, for to reduce God to our capacity, to be able to "comprehend the Almighty," is to abolish Him. So long as He is God He must be beyond us and our understanding.

Religion thus interprets the presence of mystery as the presence of God, and accounts for it in God's infiniteness.

3. The function of Religion on its practical side is to bring the soul into fellowship and harmony with the God who dwells in the mystery; to bring it into vital relation with the spiritual Reality. It is to be the medium through which the spiritual forces may enter the soul and quicken it into vigorous life.

You cannot define God, but you can open your heart to the Spirit of God. Religion, therefore, is not the accurate defining of God and the correct analysing of His Being in creed or theology, but it is the life of God dominant in the soul.

You cannot exhaust His thought, but you can trace His Will as it manifests itself in conscience and fulfil it. Religion, therefore, is not the construction of " schemes " which shall account for all the phenomena of the world and the soul, but it is the doing of the Will of God from the heart. You cannot reach forward to the ultimate purpose of God, but you can be swayed by His spirit in the direction which He indicates. Religion, therefore, is not the making of dogmatic assertions about the future which tolerate no difference of opinion, but is the reverent accord of the soul with—

> That God, which ever lives and loves,
> One God, one law, one element,
> And one far-off Divine event
> To which the whole creation moves.

THE PLACE OF REASON IN A RELIGION OF MYSTERY

CHAPTER II

THE PLACE OF REASON IN A RELIGION OF MYSTERY

WE have seen that Religion is, in its very nature, full of the element of the mysterious; it has its origin in the emergence in our consciousness of that element, and fulfils much of its function in the atmosphere created by mystery. We have in Religion, as in life, to walk much by faith, because sight fails us.

But we must be careful to guard ourselves against a possible misunderstanding, viz., that because Religion is mysterious it is therefore irrational; that its truths cannot be reasoned about, that religious faith is just believing blindly something for which we have no evidence or which such evidence as we have seems to contradict, that it is a mark of a truly religious nature to believe the unbelievable and impossible; that in Religion we have to repudiate the intelligence, the reasoning powers, the laws of Evidence, which we use in considering the facts of nature and of human life.

This is a very common misconception. There is a tendency to swing round from one extreme to the other, and, if we reject the view that Religion should answer all questions, should solve all mysteries, to refuse to recognize any place in it for the exercise of Reason. We must neither ask questions nor expect answers, or at any rate we must not hesitate to accept such answers as may be given us. Religious Faith is conceived as something opposed to and irreconcilable with Reason. To speak of a "rational Religion" is regarded as a dangerous, and indeed an irreligious, use of terms. Reason, it is said, belongs to the sphere of the intellectual, Faith to the sphere of the spiritual, and we must keep each strictly to its proper sphere.

This point of view is held by many pious and saintly people ; it suggests, when it is sincerely held, an attitude of deep reverence, and reverence always appeals to the finer side of manhood. But reverence based on a misconception, in spite of its fine appeal, ends in its own self-destruction, and leads to a state of things fatal to the development and power of Religion. That is what has happened in this case ; many great and sad evils have followed from this mistaken point of view.

We have as a result of it, for instance, the tyranny of Authority, where Church and Priest insist that we must not reason about matters of faith but must accept without question the dogmas they put before us. If we say we do not understand them, or that as far as we do understand they conflict with our Reason, " What do you expect ? " we are answered ; " Religion is a mystery, you cannot bring its truths to the test of Reason, you must accept and believe on the authority of the Church, it is want of faith to question; that is the initial heresy." This is the great confidence-trick which Authority has played upon the human soul, sheltering itself behind the essential mystery of Religion.

Or again, as a result of the point of view which shuts the Reason out of Religion we get those weak and fantastic forms of Religion, in which faith is used as a kind of narcotic to drug the soul into a spiritual hysteria, to the weakening of character and the development of a morbidity closely akin to madness. Religion so often breaks down and becomes either superstition or atheism, because of this exclusion of Reason from its sphere.

We need to be quite clear upon this matter, for clear views of the legitimate place of Reason in Religion are essential if it is to be sane and strong and of any real use.

Is there no room for faith in matters of human life and in the world of nature? Of course there is room. Our knowledge of the material, the external world, is only partial and very limited. We have seen that it is enfolded in and penetrated by mystery. We have to walk in relation to the physical world much by faith. We make our arrangements for to-morrow, but it is only in faith that to-morrow's sun will rise and we shall be here to take part in to-morrow's life. The great doctrine of Evolution upon which modern Science is built up is still largely a matter of faith, it is still full of mystery, there are many questions in relation to it which still remain unanswered, yet we build on it all the same. Into the commonest day's life the weft of faith and mystery is woven, else the warp of the known and understandable would be but a tangle of loose threads always, and never grow to fabric in the loom of time.

And yet we reason about this faith-wrought life of fact. We do not say, because into the daily experience there come the elements of faith and mystery we must therefore banish Reason. They exist side by side, and, merging the one into the other, do their work together. Though life is full of the unknown, our knowledge increases; the mystery of to-day is by the strenuous thoughts of men made plainer on the morrow; the broken and fugitive gleams of light that leap from the reverent minds of men, may be focussed on some dim region of the silent land of mystery, till in the steady light it yields its secret, widening the circle of the known, but in the act widening also, and much more, the horizon of the unknown. The Reason in solving Mystery and resolving Faith into sight does not destroy either, it only enlarges the receding horizon of the one, and creates a larger demand for the other. It makes the ultimate Mystery more marvellous, and gives to Faith a wider field, a higher flight, a deeper base.

We do not in the affairs of the material, set up a fence round the region of the unknown and warn off the trespassing intellect; rather, the realization of the mystery is ever an invitation to the intellect to explore, and the promise of a growing beauty and glory to be revealed.

And it is exactly the same in Religion. Faith and Reason can live and work together in helpful co-operation in the external and physical region, why should they not live and work together in the spiritual? If in the material world, Faith to-day becomes sight to-morrow and still leaves Faith extending beyond sight, why should it not be so in Religion? When Religion utters its great word that the mystery of life is the spiritual side of things manifesting itself, that the element of the mysterious is the manifestation of God, why should we say that Reason has no more that it can do? When in the realm of the natural world we find some strange and inexplicable thing our alert minds seek to win its secret, to know the unknown. Then when Religion changes the name and calls the mystery "God," why should we cast aside the tools of the mind and say, "Reverence forbids that we should presume further?"

There is no "thus far and no further" in the things of God. To seek to know God is not sacrilege, it is the homage the earnest mind pays to the necessary God. We need not conclude that the man who in Athens reared his altar to the unknown God built it out of the shattered fragments of his shrine to Reason; it did not mark the end of his search after the hidden God, the despairing abandonment of his quest; it was rather the first step in a new departure, the advanced outpost of a daring discoverer. So then the presence of mystery in Religion, the demand for Faith in its exercise, does not banish the Reason from that sacred realm as a rude and irreverent trespasser, as having no function to fulfil and therefore without right to interfere. God is inexhaustible. He cannot be "found out to perfection," the depths of His Being are far beyond the reach of our longest plummet line; that only gives to the reverent mind the wider scope, provides a field for its exercise worthy of its great powers, and justifies the Reason in refusing the fetters which Authority would impose to stay its progress and hinder its free activity.

But that is not the end of the matter. The exercise of the Reason in matters of faith is not only a privilege, it is a duty. In questions of the seen and temporal we hold the idle, uninquiring mind in contempt; the man who will never take the trouble to find out for himself and is content to be spoon-fed with facts which others have gathered, who never feels the bracing effect of inquiry, remains undeveloped, his power of thought decays, he never grows out of intellectual babyhood, he has no standing amongst men of strenuous mind; he is a shirker, a wastrel on one side of his nature, and the contempt in which he is held is well deserved.

And the same thing holds in questions of Religion, in matters of Faith, and in a much greater degree as the issues involved are greater, and the interests closer and more compelling. To think, to reason, to seek to know for ourselves, to wrestle with the mysteries of the spiritual world—this is the inevitable duty as it is the inalienable birthright of manhood. The man who, in imagined deference to God and at the bidding of Authority, refuses to reason about the things of God, who hands his Reason over to some third party, to Church or Priest, and accepts unquestioningly from one or the other what he is to believe and what to reject, is bartering his birthright for nothing, is burying his God-given talent, and dishonours the God Who gave it to him.

Jesus told us that to enter His kingdom we must become as little children. That means, we are told, among other things, we must as children forbear to question; we must do as we are bidden; must accept the truth as we are taught it and obey.

But we need no other justification for the clamant Reason in Religion than this word of our Teacher's. Is it characteristic of the child-mind to accept the statements of authority without bringing those statements to the arbitrament of its Reason ? Any one who has familiar knowledge of the child nature knows it is not so. The child hears, and then by an irresistible impulse asks itself "Why ?" Long after authority has given its word it is tested and tried in the child's mind and has judgment passed upon it by that searching tribunal ; an immature but remorseless and often illuminating logic is brought to bear upon it ; the child is never satisfied until it has tested and is able to express in the terms of its own experience whatever an external authority offers for its acceptance. The admonition of Jesus that we should cultivate the child attitude, applied to the relative place which Reason should occupy in Religion works out in this way : it rules out the passive, unquestioning acceptance of Truth on Authority ; it demands the serious, earnest turning over of Truth by the eager and inquiring mind, a mind restrained by humility, but alert and exacting in its intense reality ;

it demands that Truth shall be expressible in terms of its own experience by the mind that contemplates it.

The easy way in which we accept Religious beliefs without thinking, at the bidding of Church or Priest or even Fashion, is in most cases due to intellectual idleness masquerading as reverence, and is our device for concealing the fact that we do not care very much about Truth, that it is too much trouble to think, or that it is not worth our while to turn from the business and the pleasure of life to the deep things of God. It is easier to give our formal acquiescence in creed and Theology and pass them by than to test and try them by Reason and Experience before giving our assent. A Religion that is too idle, too narrowed and limited by intruding considerations of business and pleasure, of money making and the winning of social distinction, to bring its belief to the test of thought and Reason, is only a low type of Atheism.

A reverence that will not allow Religion to plead its cause, to assert its claim upon the mind as well as upon the heart, pays a poor compliment to the holy things it reveres, and evidences a poor estimate of their power. A Faith that shrinks from the calm and reverent tests of Reason is not great enough for man as God has made him.

Gathering up the threads of our thought we see :—

Religion, though inexhaustively mysterious (being the response of the soul to the manifestation of the inexhaustible God) must be Rational. God has given us our reasoning faculties and has so ordered our life on its material side that Faith and Reason have to work together to make life effective. The same principle of co-operation must be carried forward to the sphere of Religion, which is the revelation of the material in its spiritual equivalents and extension. Else the spiritual would contradict the material, which is impossible since God is consistent.

Though the mystery of God at any time extends far beyond the limits of Reason, yet it must be in accord with and fulfil the tests of Reason in so far as the mind is at any time able to overtake it. There is no Authority which can rightfully absolve the Reason of its function, much less prohibit its legitimate exercise. For any man to be justified in accepting the bare assertion of Authority he is bound to conduct a previous inquiry into the qualifications of the Authority; which is far beyond the knowledge and ability of the average man. He is less likely to go wrong in the direct and personal application of his independent Reason to the mystery of God and matters of faith than in conducting an adequate and justifying inquiry into the qualifications of the usurping Authority. The road through the Church to Truth is not a short cut: it is, if faithfully travelled, so long a journey and so full of pitfalls that few, if any, can reach the goal. The direct and independent inquiry of the individual mind in regard to the things of God is a safer, surer, shorter road to Truth than the method of verifying the Church's claims to an infallible promulgation of Truth.

To exercise the Reason with which He has endowed us is God's demand upon us, as He demands individual earnestness and sincerity from us in seeking after Him. That great and ennobling gift of His we may safely trust, if we exercise it with reverence and godly fear, to lead us daily nearer to the glorious vision of His Face. We can never hope, we need never desire to fathom the Mystery of His Being, to reach the utmost limit of His thought and purposes; but led by the reverent reasoning of the mind the horizon of the mystery may widen out and be cast in a larger circle; day by day the hidden things be made plain, the mysteries which have been secret from the foundation of the world may be revealed to the children of the Kingdom: their eyes seeing, and their ears hearing, and their hearts conceiving the things which God hath prepared for them that love Him.

THE LIMITATIONS OF REASON IN THE SPHERE OF RELIGION

CHAPTER III

THE LIMITATIONS OF REASON IN THE SPHERE OF RELIGION

REASON asserts its claim to exercise its function in the sphere of Religion, to test the conclusions of Faith by its standard, to go hand in hand with Faith through the wonder-land of mystery, to guide and discipline Faith in the exploration of that land : it is to Faith what strategy is to the soldier's martial prowess and patriotic ardour. And this claim is confirmed by a reference to what is evident and incontestable in the Order of God in other spheres of human life and experience.

But again, we must guard ourselves against misconception ; lest in the exploration of

God's wonder-land of mystery we give to Reason a dominancy which does not rightly belong to it, an infallibility which is as unjustifiable as the infallibility of Church or Creed. The function of Reason is not a despotism. There are in the philosophy of the soul's fulfilment of itself "intimations" of Truth too subtle and ethereal to be caught and focussed by the mind; there is a logic of emotion, a spiritual instinct which carries us far beyond the lagging steps of the intellect into the heart of the mystery of God. There is an atmosphere in Religion to which the Reason has to accommodate itself if its results are to be effective: it must obey the law which obtains in the sphere in which it claims to exercise its function. There are other elements of manhood which have a legitimate place in the Religious life, and it must do its work in accord with these and with fullest recognition of their claim.

The reasoning faculties cannot be disengaged from the individual; they are part of him and are conditioned by his peculiar characteristics; prejudice, educational and racial bias, temperament.

Men often speak about the Reason as though it were some arbitrary and separate instrument which does its work automatically and acts independently of the mind which employs it, as though it were some perfect self-acting machine entirely unaffected by the conditions under which it comes into operation; a kind of intellectual foot-rule—which measures true whoever handles it. So it is imagined in bringing Religion to its test the result will always and in all cases be invariable, mechanical, universally the same and beyond the possibility of error or question.

But there is no such thing as Objective Reason; it is after all entirely subjective, a function of the individual, imperfect, variable, prejudiced, affected by conditions external to itself. The test of Reason is not the application of an intellectual foot-rule, but just the man thinking, and the test will be no more reliable, no more certain in its result than the intellectual capacity of the man who applies it.

The mind must always have a horizon ; it is only Godhead that sees Truth whole. However firm the man's grip of knowledge, yet the validity of his intellectual conclusion is limited to the knowledge he possesses. There is always a region beyond his horizon, where things may be different, where the impossible may become possible, where the unimagined may be realized. He may have his surmises about what lies beyond the horizon, but in the region of surmises the mind loses its accent of confidence, and hesitates to pronounce its judgments. The writ of Reason does not run beyond the horizon of knowledge and experience, outside the borders of the realm it has conquered and made its own. It is limited in its scope to the outlook of the man who thinks.

Even within the scope of its operations the Reason is as fallible as the man is imperfect or careless. The man thinking is apt to think wrongly, to miss his way, to leave out of count factors in the case essential to its proper consideration, his mental equipment may be deficient, his logical sequences defective.

Though he test and measure with absolute sincerity, his tests may be imperfect, his measuring line inaccurate, his results unreliable. There is no such thing possible as intellectual infallibility even within the narrowest range.

St. Paul brought to the consideration of the Faith a master's intellect: powerful, swift subtle, highly trained, keen, and penetrative, a weapon of finest temper. Yet, as we follow his reasoning, it is plain to see how his bias of training and race and temperament, his strong individuality, his characteristic point of view influenced and determined his conclusions; and history has shown that when Paul carried his reasoning processes beyond the limits of knowledge and experience, his surmises, as in the case of the speedy second coming of the Lord, were mistaken. The creed of

Nicæa is no more or less infallible than the fallibility of the Fathers of the Church in Council assembled. The student who knows the history and conditions of the age from which it came can recognize in its clauses the characteristic tendencies, the intellectual peculiarities and limitations of the men who framed it.

The intellectual test which any Church or individual applies to Faith is always conditioned by the intellectual capacities and peculiarities of the individual or the Church.

It will never be quite identical in its results in any two individuals or in any two periods of the Church's history, unless it be possible to imagine that there can be absolute similarity in all the subtle factors that contribute to the intellectual processes of the two individuals or an absolute arrestment of the Church's life between the two periods.

Since then, in the nature of things, the Reason, however essential its exercise in the search for Faith, can never be an absolute and infallible guide; since there is no such thing as Objective Reason, which is independent of the mind that exercises it, since it is nothing more or less than the man thinking, and must be affected and its results determined by the individual characteristics of the man who thinks, there are certain practical considerations which should always be kept clearly in view in our reasoning about matters of Religion and problems of Faith.

1. There can be no finality about our intellectual conclusions.

It is often thought that the doctrines of the Church are to be accepted as the complete and final statement of Truth, which can never suffer any change, never grow outworn, never be inadequate, which must always be accepted by the faithful, the questioning of which is something akin to blasphemy.

Doctrine thus hardens into dogma. We confuse doctrine with Truth; but Truth, which is of God, must always be greater than doctrine, which is of man and therefore subject to the limitations of the man who frames it. The doctrines of the Church are only the forms in which have been stated conceptions of Truth; the human vessel, which contains, but does not exhaust, the truth of God! The Truth remains, but our conception of it may vary, grow wider and deeper. The formation of doctrine is the result of a complex activity within the personality; will, feeling, thought, all contribute to its production. It is not intellectual alone, but is the resultant of Truth taken up into the personality, subjected to the play of the subtle forces of the assimilating personality, and emerging again deeply marked and coloured by the forces that have played upon it. It must therefore be subject to all the limitations of the source from which it comes. It may be the adequate expression of Truth as conceived by any one age or individual, but if there be any increase of knowledge, any development of intellectual capacity, any possibility of changing the point of view, not to say any purification of emotion and ennoblement of the will, it follows that the doctrines of the Church not only may, but must, be constantly changing their form, readjusting their outlook, varying their emphasis ; stepping stones of our living selves to higher things, and milestones which mark our progress toward the ultimate reality. And this necessary tentativeness of doctrine, this non-finality of our intellectual conception of Truth, opens out wide possibilities for us. We feel, at any time, if we are humble, the inadequacy of our view of truth. We are often perplexed and stand helpless before the apparent contradictions of life, our Reason often throws us upon the horns of a dilemma which seems inevitable. The best we can think, the clearest statement of our thoughts is unsatisfactory and vague. Then we are glad to remember our limitations, to remember the horizon. The tangled threads of thought and reason may be straitened out beyond ; the irreconcilable sets of facts, as they seem to be here, may find their reconciliation there; laws which seem to conflict here may be seen to be merged in some higher law when the horizon widens. No doctrine is complete or final in itself: it has long tendrils of suggestion which stretch out into the unexplored region of the unknown. So, although as it stands, and as far as it carries us, it may be sound, yet it mostly involves other things which are not resolved, and these when they are resolved may modify the doctrine out of which they have sprung.

2. There must always be a certain diffidence in the application of Reason to Religion, a humbling and restraining sense of the limitations and inadequacy of the instrument we are using, of our inability to see all, or always to see clearly and in proper perspective. An over confident and braggart intellectualism in religion has perhaps been the cause of more error and mischief to the soul than an unreasoning superstition. For Reason to be an effective aid to us in exploring the mysterious region of the unknown, or in sur-

veying accurately the land that is already open, a necessary condition is that we should exercise it diffidently and with a definite realization of its limitations and fallibility. If this condition is observed we shall then be susceptible to the incoming of fresh light; we shall be prepared for re-adjustments consequent upon clearer vision or increasing knowledge; there will be no blinding finality about our thoughts, progress in the soul's pilgrimage Godward will be steady and secure.

3. With the realization of the inherent imperfections of our reasoning faculties there will come to the earnest seeker after the Truth of God, the resolute endeavour to make them as effective as possible, to train our minds to correct and careful thinking.

Perhaps in no department of life and experience do men so play fast and loose with thought, are so careless in their thought, or think so little, as in Religion. It is so easy to take things for granted and it seems to make no difference. It is by some actually regarded as a virtue to do no thinking at all in this which is, if there be any sincerity in Religion, the supremest interest of life.

Careless thinking, loose reasoning, is the sign of an indolent nature, and indolence in the things of God indicates an indifference, and perhaps contempt, more hurtful to the soul than the unbelief in which an earnest thinker sometimes goes astray. With a deep consciousness of the greatness of the issues involved, and the, at best, imperfect tools of the mind with which we have to fashion our thoughts into life-giving belief, we shall take care so to use our tools, so to train and discipline thought, as to get the best results possible.

4. The Reason is a function of the individual; it is therefore marked with the peculiarities of the individual, and its results are affected by them. But it is just this element of individuality, with all its imperfections, that makes belief so precious. Whatever its limitations, its partial view of things,

it is his, the man's own, and he must live by it; another man's belief is no use to him. The thing he thinks, the view of Truth to which he has by his own careful and earnest thought won his way, is for him the essentially true thing—to it he must give his entire loyalty. It is this personal appropriation of Truth that makes our belief effective. The working value of a belief is not determined solely by its relative truthfulness, but by its close and vital relation to the man who holds it. The most perfect creed which may be presented to us is not so helpful to our life as the far cruder conceptions which we have fashioned for ourselves, and which are the product of our own experience and thought.

Even Truth is dear bought at the price of individuality, for Truth apart from a personal experience of it becomes a lie.

5. So we come to understand how absurd and presumptuous it is to endeavour to force the results of our reasoning processes upon others, or to expect other minds to accept our

dicta as of final authority. Such an acceptance would be worth nothing and less than nothing; it would be harmful to the accepting mind. The man upon whom a Church or an individual forces conclusions is shut out from that personal appropriation of Truth which can only come by free inquiry and individual effort. The doctrines we hold can be really our own only as they are the product of a process in the heart and mind of the man who holds them, a process in which the facts upon which the doctrines are based are absorbed into the personality, and emerge in a form which accurately expresses the results of the process. Other minds may guide and suggest, but the resulting doctrine must bear the stamp of individuality. Lacking this personal element—that is, if the doctrine be forced upon us by, or borrowed from, some source external to ourselves, it can have no reality, no vital power; it stands for nothing within the man, it represents no personal appropriation of Truth; it represents nothing but a great act of tyranny or a demoralized and demoralizing idleness.

That the Church says this or that, that this or that great doctrine has won the acceptance of generations of pious souls, demands for it our respect, our careful inquiry ; but it cannot demand our acceptance until we feel that it is the adequate expression of thoughts which are our own.

Otherwise we sacrifice our sincerity, and all that makes Truth precious, simply to be on the side of the majority.

6. And finally, when we clearly perceive the necessary and inevitable independence of the individual Reason in matters of Religion we are in a position to appreciate the relation and value of the individual mind to the common Faith. Independence does not mean isolation. Freedom in isolation is Anarchy, and Anarchy carried to its logical end involves mutual destruction. It has been a favourite trick of Authority to call personal liberty Anarchy, and so to justify its en-

deavour to destroy liberty. But just as in the State, so in Religion, there is a personal independence which is not only compatible with the common bond of community, but essential to its fulfilment.

The Reason may be free and unfettered in its activity, and the result of that free activity be to add to the common treasure of knowledge, to give to the common Faith a firmer foundation and a wider scope. The larger the liberty of all to test and try, the larger and surer the results will be. The greater the number of free explorers in the realm of nature, the richer grows our store of knowledge. That is equally true in the sphere of the spiritual Reason is in its very nature individual, and reflects in its operation and its results the individuality of the mind ; then the freer the scope that is allowed to the Reason the richer, more varied, more human and universal will be the common product of knowledge and faith to which such varied and universal types of mind contribute.

The best results have been won, the noblest and strongest life of Faith has been lived, not in the ages when the dead hand of Authority has rigidly presented the limits and direction in which the individual Reason may work, but in the ages when the Thoughts of men have been unfettered, when every man has had the fullest liberty to exercise his birthright of Reason. A strong State is a State whose citizens are free; a strong and true Faith is a Faith whose disciples are free. A communism that crushes out the individuality of its members is self-destructive. A common Faith that is built up by the free inquiry, by the independent Reason of the individual, will have the most universal appeal, the largest outlook, the richest store of Treasure and the most enduring results.

RELIGION AND EXPERIENCE

CHAPTER IV

THE ULTIMATE PROOF OF RELIGION LIES IN SPIRITUAL EXPERIENCE

ALL that has preceded prepares us for the appreciation of the truth which is stated as the heading of the present chapter.

The Reason has its place and its work in Religion, but under certain inevitable limitations.

It may state and test and correct the expressions of Religious Truth; but it moves in a world greater than itself, a world, the phenomena of which transcend the intellectual faculty. The facts of Religion may be stated in terms of the intellect, and must be so stated if belief is to be practical and communicated. But the facts of Religion are, after all, not intellectual but spiritual, and, for the individual at any rate, the full appreciation of (producing an effective faith in) those spiritual facts is to be achieved not by means of the intellectual faculties, but by the direct contact of the spiritual faculties with the spiritual facts in the region of experience.

The absolutely satisfying and final assertion of religious truth lies not in the mind but in the soul. It is a thing, not of creeds and theologies, but of vision and knowledge. The aim of the present chapter is to make this clear.

It is one of the hopeful signs of the times that people are now more anxious, than was formerly the case, to find "a reason for the hope that is in them," to establish Faith on the broad base of personal knowledge, rather than upon the doubtful foundation of Authority. There is a desire for such reality and intensity in faith as can only come to one as the result of personal experience. There is less disposition to take things for granted, less contentment with a Faith possessed only by inheritance and not by personal effort and realization.

"What do I really believe, and why do I believe it?" These questions find an echo in many hearts and minds to-day. No one can be at all familiar with the story of Religion during the present generation, or with the atmosphere in which Religion lives, and not be conscious of the spirit of inquiry which pervades them. There is a fearless and eager resoluteness in inquiry which fifty years ago was not to be found.

For this the lover of Faith, the seeker after God, should be devoutly thankful; for although in the process of inquiry there is a very general reconstruction necessary, and many elements in the previously accepted beliefs are discarded, yet the resulting faith is far more precious because more personal; more real, and therefore more effective in the character and life.

Of course, one must not imagine that this

eagerness to test and prove the validity of faith is universal. There is still much of prejudice to be broken down, much natural timidity lest in casting off the old moorings the currents of thought should carry one on to a pitiful shipwreck of Faith; and this timidity has to be overcome.

There are still very many who are willing to take over their beliefs without testing or even understanding them, and still many who are too idle or indifferent to think for themselves; there are some remaining who quite sincerely regard "faith" and "proof" as irreconcilable, to whom the endeavour to "prove the things not seen" is, in spite of the author of the Epistle to the Hebrews, a futile and dangerous proceeding.

But this attitude is slowly though surely giving place to the other. People are waking up to the necessity of knowing what and why they believe. There is an increasing desire to possess a faith which is not outside the necessity for proof, but which becomes a necessity by reason of its being proved.

But just at this point a difficulty arises; a difficulty which is sure to arise in such circumstances of awakening as we have described. A question has to be faced, and answered on right lines, if we are to achieve that convincing attestation of our belief which so many are seeking. How can I prove the truth of the things I believe? What is to be the convincing argument by which my soul shall be assured of the reality of God, of Jesus Christ, of the saving power of the Gospel of Jesus? What is the proper line of inquiry along which I shall be able to verify my religion, in what direction am I to look for its justification?

That is the question of first and main importance for all who are in earnest in these matters. Upon its clear and intelligent answer depends the final outcome of inquiry.

It is from this point that many, taking the wrong road, find themselves landed either in a Faith that lacks reality and effectiveness or in a despairing scepticism. There is only one way that leads to conviction, and peace and power; only one safe road for the inquirer to travel. Other roads from this point, though they seem to be direct and speedy, are either mere cul-de-sacs, or they are full of pitfalls, and along them lurk many foes to Faith, against which the unwary traveller all unprepared falls an easy prey to unbelief.

Let us try to answer this question at once, and state the principle which, when it is understood, and all it involves appreciated, will save us from many mistakes, rid us of many difficulties, and open a plain path for us to arrive at a satisfying conviction of the truth of our religion and the power of our Christian Faith. The principle is very simple and quite obvious, viz., *That Religion being essentially personal and having to do with spiritual things, the ultimate proof of religious truth lies in the spiritual experience of the individual.*

Let us see what this involves, and what it excludes, a not unimportant consideration.

A great many so-called "evidences" of religion, and of Christianity in particular, are entirely inadequate. Logically they may be perfect, but there are other elements needful for conviction besides flawless logic. Such "evidences" are all very well as far as they go, they may be usefully taken as subsidiary lines of attestation confirming the main argument, but they lie outside the spiritual region, their value is at the mercy of many considerations which are entirely external to the spiritual issue; as, for example, the intellectual ability to follow them, or one's cleverness in stating them correctly. Links in the chain of evidence which they make may be flawed or missing, and so the chain be weakened to the point of uselessness. And above all many of them lie outside the realm of personal experience, and are correspondingly of little power in the personal life; they make a poor appeal to the individual conscience, and Religion has most to do with conscience ; unless the seat of its power and authority be there it cannot possibly be effective in any real sense—the conviction of religion must depend upon its appeal to conscience.

Let us take an example of this inadequate evidence.

There is the argument for the existence of God based upon what is called the evidence of design, i.e. the witness to the presence of a supreme and dominating Intelligence to be found in the world of nature. That is a very strong argument in its own line. It is difficult to imagine how any sane mind can look at nature with all its marvels of adjustment and correspondence and escape the conviction of the existence of an infinite Intelligence behind and in nature. The whole drift of scientific investigation is to illustrate and deepen that conviction. The closer and more accurate our knowledge the more impossible does it become to escape it.

This argument from design is only one of many similar, in other directions, to prove not only God's existence, but His wisdom, power, goodness, and love. They are all open to the same objections. They do not of necessity appeal to our own knowledge, their data lie often outside the spiritual region, they do not touch the conscience, they may not appeal to anything within our spiritual experience. The argument from design depends for its force very largely upon a close and accurate knowledge of the facts and forces of the physical world, and the average man does not possess such knowledge. To appreciate fully its significance we need to have a knowledge, wide in its range and minute in its detail, a keen logical faculty, and much beside of the same kind. If we have these then the argument has considerable force as a piece of reasoning, but does not necessarily possess an equal force of spiritual appeal. If we have them not then it fails even to carry our Reason ; or at best we have to accept it on the authority of those who know, and in Religion "Authority" is ever an ineffective ground of faith. We ought to believe in God, not because certain clever people, who know a great deal, out of their knowledge tell us that there are such and such facts which prove the existence of God ; we ought to believe in God because we have realized His presence in our own experience.

So, deeply and wearily conscious of the inadequacy of all such arguments which lie in the purely logical and external region, arguments which, however clear in their reasoning and unassailable in their facts, leave the heart untouched and the soul unsatisfied, we come to our principle that the ultimate proof of religion lies in spiritual experience. The supreme proof to our hearts (and it is only to our hearts that Religion can be effectively proved) lies not in the argument from design, or the supremacy of law, or anything of that order, it lies in the spiritual experience of the heart. The felt necessity of our souls for someone higher than ourselves, the tragic hunger and thirst of the Soul for God, this is what convinces our hearts of the inevitability of God. This is the argument from design carried forward into the region of spiritual experience.

Then, when the soul finds its necessity met, its hunger and thirst satisfied in communion with and dependence on the God whom Jesus reveals to us: when, in high moments of fellowship with Him whose existence is not logically proved by a series of deductions but seized by spiritual intuition, there enters the soul a peace which passes all understanding, a sense of satisfaction which is inexhaustible, a joy which thrills all our being, an uplifting inspiration which fills the life with power—*then* God becomes to us an indestructible Reality. It is by these personal spiritual experiences that we become "very sure of

God." When a man or woman has passed through them, has heard the still small voice of God in the heart; has felt the touch of God's Spirit quickening into life and activity all that is fine and holy within; when the law of God in conscience has been realized, and in moments of meditative apartness the vision of the Father's face has dawned upon the wrapt soul, then His Reality is most surely experienced. In such moments as these we come to know Him in Whom we believe.

This internal witness to God is, of course, essentially personal and is incapable of being made, in any particular instance, equally forceful and real to those who are external to the individual that experiences it. But Religion is at the bottom a personal thing, its appeal is to the individual and reaches the individual not in the experiences of other souls, but in what the individual has seen and felt.

There is this also to be said. If the proof of religion lies chiefly in the spiritual experiences of the individual, *that proof is unassailable from without.* The critic of faith may riddle with his arguments the formal and external "proofs" of God, he may detect flaws in the logic by which God is demonstrated, but you go on your way untouched by his criticism for he has not seen what you have seen, he has not heard the things which you have heard. Has not the vision of the Father's face been unveiled before you, has not the still small voice of the Eternal sounded in your heart! The face and the voice are facts in your experience; what does he know of these? But *you* know, and you can laugh at his attempt to deny spiritual facts which are as sure to you at least, as are the "facts" of the physical world. He may have the advantage of you in logic and reasoning, but you have seen, you have heard, you have felt, therefore you know. If he has not entered into your experience he cannot deny the facts of your experience, at any rate his denial will have no validity for you.

The same argument holds with equal force in regard to the Christian Faith. Most people are more or less acquainted with the common lines of evidence for the Truth of Christianity. Splendid work has been done by a long succession of Christian Apologists, who have endeavoured to base the proof of the Christian Faith on external evidence and formal logic.

There is the historical evidence for the life and teaching of Jesus ;—that He really lived in Galilee, and said and did the things recorded in the Gospels. No historical event has been so closely scrutinized as the life of Jesus, and no documents have ever been subjected to such searching and hostile criticisms as the New Testament writings ; and in spite of minor modifications which do not affect the main issue, they emerge triumphantly from each new phase of the process. It is now only the Editor of some popular Journal, innocent of Scholarship or effective knowledge which qualifies to give a final judgment, who will venture airily to dismiss the record as historically worthless.

There are the evidences to be gathered from the history of the Early Church and the first centuries of the Faith; the evidence of a countless host of witnesses who have tried the Gospel and have lived by its power.

There is the argument from miracles, which appeals with great force to some minds; an argument which not so long ago was held in low repute, but which is once again acquiring force from the facts urged by the new Psychology, and in the relation which Psychologists are suggesting between the physical and the psychical spheres of personality.

These and other veins of evidence have been worked with rich results to the establishment of Christianity on a sure foundation of formal demonstration.

But when all is said and done, it has to be acknowledged that, though these have their place and value, they are inadequate. They do not provide the supreme and final proof, valid for the individual heart and conscience, of the truth of the Gospel. It is not by these that the Christian Faith is made effective. They are all external to our own experience, they lie outside our life. We may not possess either the knowledge or the logical faculty to grasp the facts or to appreciate the argument built on them. We probably have to take them as granted, second-hand and on the authority of those who know; this may be perfectly legitimate but it may leave the conscience untouched. And again it must be urged that for religion to be effective as a dominant force it must appeal not to knowledge and the Reason only, but to the heart and the conscience. It is possible to grasp the facts and follow the argument upon which Christianity is formally demonstrated and yet to leave both heart and conscience untouched, and faith unrealized. And Faith that rests upon these external proofs only is open to assault on every hand. Its defence depends on knowledge and the critical faculty and intellectual acuteness—failing the possession of these it may easily be shattered. If a man have no surer ground for the Christian hope upon which his life is built than the historical argument and formal logic he may wake up one morning and find his Faith in ruins and his life and hope wrecked.

In which direction then are we to look for the most convincing proof of the truth and power of the Gospel, and the validity of our Faith? Again our principle comes to our aid and suggests the answer:—in our own personal experience. We believe the Gospel of Jesus, ultimately, not because the documents are proved authentic and the event historical, not because miracles happened, not even because others have lived by the Faith, but because we can live by it, and live best by it; because, when once we have tried it, we cannot live without it. We believe in the Gospel of Jesus because we find its ideals worthiest of our manhood, because it lifts us highest. We believe in Jesus as our Saviour, because He does, in our own experience, save us from our sins, and not because of any theological scheme of Salvation. We believe in Him as the great Reconciler because He does bring us into at-one-ment with God, and not because of any Theory of the Atonement. We believe in His divinity because in Him we have ourselves seen the very brightness of the Father's Glory. We believe in Him as our Guide because, following Him, we have been led on from glory to glory. He has brought hope to us in hours of depression ; His words have flashed new and radiant significance upon human life and destiny. We have felt His presence with us in times of sorrow and distress bringing peace and quietness.

These and a thousand other experiences in which we have come into vital communion with Him, in which we have felt His power, and our lives have been glorified by the realization of His presence, these are the supreme proof to us of the truth and power of the Gospel of Jesus.

No man gives as his reason for eating bread that the chemical analysis of it proves its fitness to sustain life, he eats it because he has found in his own experience its satisfying and sustaining qualities. So we feed our souls on the Bread of Life come down from God, not because by argument and logic this or that is proved about Him, but because we have partaken of that Bread and have proved that He gives to us the highest and finest life of the Soul,—Eternal Life. This is the sure and certain ground of our hope and faith in Christ, this personal experience, this knowledge of what He has actually done and is doing for us. And how unassailable it is from without. What is all the artillery of criticism to us! Why need we disturb ourselves if the Johannine authorship of the fourth Gospel be proved impossible;—nay, a reverent criticism must have its perfect work;

let in the streams of light, of historic investigation, of critical analysis, let us by all means know how matters stand with the documents. What does it matter? For the supreme witness to the truth of the Christian message lies not even in Gospel or Epistle, but it lies in the living characters of the Book of our own life, whose secret pages none other than ourselves can read; the Evangel is written plain and unmistakable before us in the Christ within.

No man is able to judge Christ till he has tried Him. No man is able to pass judgment on the truth and value of the Gospel till he has tried to live by it. It is this which in a sentence sweeps away all the arguments which are urged by professed unbelievers.

Whatever value the Christian apologetic on the older lines may have within its own sphere, with whatever of historical knowledge and forensic skill the documents of the New

Testament and the doctrines of the Catholic Faith may be defended and enforced, it becomes more and more inevitable that the final reason for the Christian hope within us must rest on the new apologetic of the personal experience of the redeeming and uplifting power of the Christ in the heart and life of the individual. " Christ in us " is the Christian's true and indestructible " hope of Glory."

THE NEW APOLOGETIC AND THE WORK OF JESUS

CHAPTER V

THE NEW APOLOGETIC AND THE WORK OF JESUS

IN the preceding chapter we dealt with the new point of view in the modern apologetic. We explained that many of the reasons for belief which had great weight with men in times past make little appeal to us to-day; not that they have been proved illogical or invalid, but because under changed conditions of thought and feeling and life, the old arguments, the old point of view, have given place to a new order of evidence and reasoning.

In the Tower of London there is an interesting collection of the weapons of offence and defence which have been used by our ancestors in fighting the battles of our native land. Most of them have no other use possible now than to repose in a Museum of Antiquities, because, although tremendously effective in their time, modern conditions of warfare have so changed as to make them useless for their original purpose.

Of what use would be the old long-bow of the sturdy yeomen, which won for us many a glorious victory, or the heavy armour of the gallant knight, against modern artillery or the long-range rifle of to-day ?

We should find very much the same thing if we were to pass through the armoury of the Christian Faith. Many of the arguments which under the then conditions of thought and feeling and experience did splendid service in urging the claims of Christianity and in defence of the Faith, under the conditions of modern times (with wider knowledge, larger experience, altered feelings) would have but little force in appealing to the reason and conscience of our time. The Cause remains the same, the same eternal Truths are at stake, but the battle-ground has changed, the weapons of the Christian soldier are different. The tactics of the foe have altered, and have to be met by a new strategy. The burning questions of a hundred years ago have burnt themselves out. The ashes of old controversies are mainly of interest as marking the historic progress of the fight, the camp fires of contending hosts. The campaign has passed into new regions. It is this fact which explains the growing dissatisfaction of the Church with certain of the creeds which were drawn to meet special conditions and to deal with special phases of thought (as witness the movement in the Anglican Church to abolish or modify the Athanasian Creed) and which lies at the root of our suspicion of all credal statements as a permanent basis of Christian Fellowship. It is not that the Faith has altered, or that the Gospel of Jesus has changed, but it is that the appeal of the Gospel reaches us along different channels ; the Faith must be a living Faith, built up out of the facts by which we are surrounded, expressed in terms of the life about us, and able to withstand the currents of criticism and unbelief which surge around it in the flood-tide of our full and complex life.

Let us further illustrate the position by one or two examples.

(A) In the controversies of a hundred years ago we find that a large part was played by the argument from miracles. In a past age men found in the miracles of Jesus one of the most convincing arguments for the Christian Faith, and opponents of the Faith endeavoured to prove that miracles did not and could not happen. But now-a-days the cautious man of Science hesitates to say what is possible or impossible, while the thoughtful disciple believes in Jesus not because of the miracles He is said to have worked, but he is inclined to believe in the miracles because Jesus wrought them. The part played in the

Faith of the Christian disciple by the miraculous element has completely altered in character.

(B) Or again, the argument from the fulfilment of prophecy; "Certain men" it was said, "centuries before Jesus appeared predicted certain things about a promised Messiah: Jesus fulfilled those predictions, therefore He was the promised Messiah." But now we understand that the main function of the prophets was to preach Righteousness to their own generation. We believe in Jesus as our Saviour, not so much because He fulfils certain predictions which came down from the dim past but because He fulfils the aspirations and longings and ideals of our own hearts.

These and similar lines of argument may be as valid as ever, but they do not interest us as keenly as they did our fathers, they do not appeal to the conscience. They are remote from the modern atmosphere. It is in the promised self-manifestation of the

Christ to the disciple that the main strength of Christian apologetic lies.

In the inner region of the heart there comes that vision of the Christ, that redeeming fellowship, those uplifting and saving impulses which the Christ in us communicates ; all of these are to us the sure and certain evidence that He is worthy to be our Saviour and Lord.

The New Apologetic is subjective in its appeal, it seeks to establish the claim of Jesus on what is found within, on the authority of the spirit of God as it speaks in and to the Soul.

As we can easily understand, this change in point of view has altered in some respects what we may call the perspective of faith. Certain elements which at one time were regarded as of first importance have lost their supreme place, while others which were held to be secondary and less important have become primary and essential.

(c) At one time it was thought to be of

essential importance that a disciple should hold certain precise and definite theological doctrines, should accept even the set form of words in which those doctrines were expressed. For a man to have his doubts about the generally received doctrines, and especially some of them, was regarded as imperilling his discipleship. Even now you sometimes find a representative of the old order saying that a man cannot be a Christian who does not believe in the philosophical doctrine of the Deity of Christ, in the legal view of the atonement, in the absolute infallibility of the Bible in all its parts.

But, generally speaking, a change has been effected in our attitude in reference to this matter. While it is still felt to be of great importance that a disciple should have clear and definite ideas, yet we do not say that it is essential to discipleship to hold certain theological dogmas. It is of more importance that we should make Jesus the dominant influence in thought and feeling and conduct than that we should accept certain intellectual statements about Him. We do not now say that the acceptance of right doctrine will lead to true discipleship, but we reverse it and say that if we try to be faithful disciples we shall under His influence be led to see Truth aright. Or as He himself put it: "If any man willeth to do his will, he shall know of the teaching whether it be of God."

(D) At one time it was thought to be essential that the disciple of Jesus should be in recognized association with the organized life of the Church. Indeed it was claimed that the graces and privileges of discipleship could only reach the individual through the channel of the Church. An effective discipleship was regarded as impossible outside the Church. There are very many who still believe that:—the Roman Church and a large section of the Anglican Church. But the modern spirit and the modern point of view are against it, as the New Testament is against it. We are beginning to realize, that while it is of great importance to the effectiveness of the Church, and, if anything, of greater importance for the culture of the individual spiritual life that all who are in sympathy with Jesus and have felt His presence and power within them, should associate themselves with the brotherhood of the disciples, yet most important of all is it that the disciple should be in close and vital communion with Jesus. Fellowship with the Christ is far more than fellowship with the Church ; it comes first in the logical order. It is not the Church that makes a man a Christian, but it is the individual disciple in close fellowship with Jesus, who makes the Church Christian.

So one might go on illustrating in many ways the change which is made in the perspective or emphasis of the Christian Faith by the recognition of this principle that the supreme ground of faith is what the individual knows of Jesus in his own personal experience.

But there is a question which suggests itself and which we must proceed to consider viz.,—If the ultimate ground for belief in Jesus is that which in our experience He is to us and does for us, what then does a faith in Him so founded mainly involve ?

1. First of all it involves that the main object in the work of Jesus for man is to effect a change of character in the individual, a change of heart. The influence of Jesus is the divine answer to the prayer breathed by all the nobler sort of human kind : "Create in me a clean heart, O God, and renew a right spirit within me." To cleanse the thought, to purify the affections, to ennoble the emotions, to lift up the desires, to strengthen the will, to clear the spiritual perception ; to teach men the evil of wrong-doing, to make them hate it, to give them the impulse and the power to fight and conquer the evil within

their own hearts ; to teach men the beauty of holiness and right-doing, to make them love it, to give them the impulse and the power to seek after it and possess it ; to teach men what God is like, to give them a true and noble vision of God, and to so influence the hearts of men as to kindle a real and deep love for God, out of which there shall grow increasingly an absorbing desire to do God's will ; to teach men to trust in God and to find in Him their strength and joy and peace ;—to accomplish all this in the inner region of the heart of man is the main purpose of Jesus.

Jesus Christ and His Gospel are concerned, in the first instance and pre-eminently, with the inward life of the individual. He did not come to organize an ecclesiastical empire like that of Rome, nor to formulate a theological system into which the whole world should force its thought, nor to lay down a set of formal rules for the external life which all men must obey. He came to make men good, to bring them to God. He came to cleanse the heart and renew the spirit, knowing full well that if He could purify the secret spring of life the whole stream would be pure ; that if the soul of the individual could be brought into harmony with God, then the external life of the individual, and of the Society, and of the Nation, and of the Race, also would be redeemed. The secret of the world's salvation lies within the heart of the individual, and it is there that Jesus does His work.

2. And secondly, it involves that we should give Him the opportunity to effect this change in us. If faith in Jesus is built up on what we know of Him, on what in our experience He does in and for us, then it is obvious that the primary fact in discipleship is not the acceptance of a creed nor the attainment of a certain standard of excellence in character, but simply and solely the willingness to give the Christ the opportunity to do His

work in us, to open the door of the heart for Him to enter in, the desire to learn of Him.

It is beginning at the wrong end to expect the would-be disciple to acquiesce in certain doctrines about Christ. How should he acquiesce in statements of which he as yet knows little or nothing? He comes to Jesus to learn the truth from Him. How can he be expected to possess the virtues and graces of the Christian life, when the very purpose of his approach to Jesus is to have those graces and virtues developed in him by the magic influence of Jesus?

"Nothing in my hand I bring" he is taught to sing, and then we expect him to pass an examination in Christian doctrine, to bring a creed, a theology "in his hand" before we recognize him as a disciple. That is an absurd reversal of the true order.

You cannot believe in Jesus till you have tried Him, tried whether He can and does accomplish in you that change of character which it is His supreme work to effect. And what is equally true is that you cannot pass any judgment upon Him, you cannot say that He is a failure, that He and His Gospel are unworthy of your faith until you have tried for yourself, in your own experience. Any estimate of Christ, whether favourable or adverse, that is not based on experience, is absolutely worthless.

His claim upon us is based on a fact which all who are not morally insane will admit, that every one ought to avail himself of every possible help towards the perfection of character. What He claims from all of us who have not repudiated manhood is that we should give Him the opportunity of achieving His work in and for us. The man or woman who yields to that claim, has entered upon the happy pilgrimage of Christian discipleship which ends in salvation and power and peace. It cannot be too plainly or too insistently proclaimed that to be a disciple of Jesus involves no pledge of doctrine, no previous perfection, but simply that, out of an earnest desire for all that is good and pure, we give Him an absolutely fair trial, we give Him an entirely unfettered opportunity; that we sincerely endeavour to live our life in the power of His presence and companionship and inspiration.

It is to the recognition of this fact that the Church must return.

If we will allow our thought to run back over the story of the past we shall see that it is in this way that the Christian Faith has won its triumphs and done its highest work.

The external glory of the Church, her power and her wealth, her conquests over emperors and kings and governments, even her logic and her learning, her philosophy and theology—in so far as these have been made the end of her activities—will all be swept on one side in the final reckoning up of accounts. Judgment will be passed upon her in so far as she has striven after and accomplished the work of persuading men to give Jesus Christ the opportunity He desires, in so far as she has opened the door of the human heart for her Lord to enter in.

Her noblest sons and daughters have been not her Popes and Cardinals, her Bishops and Priests, but those saintly ones who by her influence have opened their hearts to the Christ, and had their manhood and womanhood redeemed by Him. Wherever He has failed the result lies not in His inadequacy, but in the inadequate opportunity afforded Him.

These are things which the Church and the world need tq ponder well. The power of this new-old appreciation of the Christ —the perception of that wherein His work truly consists—contains within it the promise and the potency of that redeemed humanity which is the dream of all who are worthy to be called men.

THE WITNESS OF HISTORY TO THE NEW APOLOGETIC

CHAPTER VI

THE WITNESS OF HISTORY TO THE NEW APOLOGETIC

THE underlying principle of the New Apologetic carries us back to the atmosphere of the first century in the story of the Church. The history of the early years is an emphatic witness to its absolute effectiveness. There we find the principle in its simplest and most evident operation. A careful inquiry into the conditions under which the Christian Faith gained its first hold upon the hearts of men makes it abundantly plain that, for the disciple of those days, the supreme and satisfying proof of the truth and power of the Gospel lay in the experience of the individual.

The amazingly rapid spread of the Christian Faith in the first century suggests the presence of some extraordinary and mysterious factor in the conditions. It is not to be explained by the facts that appear on the surface. Try to account for the marvel of the first century, to get at its secret, and we find that its secret lies in this, the power and presence of the Christ realized in the experience of the individual.

In this chapter we shall consider some of the circumstances that point to this conclusion, we shall try to find the historic witness to the validity of the New Apologetic.

In reading those portions of the four Gospels which tell of the closing scenes of Christ's earthly ministry, it is evident that Jesus perfectly well understood how unprepared His disciples were for the great work that lay before them in the future. Though He had been with them for three years teaching and guiding them they were still in the lower class of the school of Christ.

They had much to learn, and much to unlearn—many old and hindering prejudices had to go before they could fully appreciate the message and ideals of Jesus. No one could have seen that more clearly than He saw it. And yet it does not seem to have disturbed or discouraged Him. With His departure shortly to be accomplished, with His disciples still far from effective for the purposes of the future He is confident about committing the Gospel to their charge.

If we read the accounts of His closing conversation with His disciples we readily perceive the ground of His confidence. He clearly looked forward to the continuation of His ministry of teaching, and His power to influence them directly and personally after the withdrawal of His visible presence from amongst them. Whether He was mistaken or not is another matter, that has to be decided on the evidence of later events, but judging from the reports of His conversations with them, as He approached the final tragedy of His betrayal and death, He unmistakably believed that He would still, in the future, be able to teach and guide and influence His disciples; that they would continue to learn from Him. "Lo, I am with you alway, even unto the end of the world." Nothing could be plainer or more emphatic than that.

Now, do we find anything in the story of the disciples, and of the early Church that seems to justify this belief? We find two very striking facts.

1. The disciples, and even those who, though not among the company with whom those conversations were held, came through their preaching to be His disciples, were firmly convinced that they were under the direct and personal inspiration and guidance of the spirit of Jesus. They absolutely believed that Jesus was still with them, guiding them in difficult matters of conduct, leading them to a fuller knowledge of Truth,

giving them needful courage in times of danger and imparting to their hearts true and right feeling. The early Christians believed Jesus was as truly in their midst as teacher and guide as He had been with the Twelve in the days of His earthly ministry. This is the only doctrine of the Real Presence which has any primitive warrant. Explain it how we may we cannot get rid of the fact, that this belief in the actual presence and continued ministry of Jesus with and to each individual disciple, was one of the main factors in the life and faith of the men and women of the first century It was real to them, and was to a very great extent the source of their devotion and courage and enthusiasm.

It may be said that it was all a delusion on their part. That is a possible objection. We simply take note of it now and go on to say, if it was a delusion then we have to find an explanation for a second striking and even more wonderful fact in the story of the first century.

2. Among the early disciples there evidently was some strange and mighty power at work, the effect of which was manifest in several directions, and the explanation of which cannot be found in the conditions which appear on the surface.

For example :—

(A) After the death of Jesus the disciples made immense and rapid progress in their spiritual education, in their perception and appreciation of the issues involved in the message of their Master. They made mistakes, they had wrong impressions ; but against all the ordinary chances, their impressions were corrected, their mistakes only led them to a truer view of things. Prejudices, which according to the usual methods and laws of human thought and feeling ought to have strengthened, were, as a matter of fact, shaken off. The point of view to which they seemed firmly fixed at the passing of Jesus was against all human calculation relinquished, and slowly but surely they moved to His own.

Their relation to Him strangely enough never had anything reminiscent about it, as one cherishes the memory of a friend who has passed from us, it always had the actuality of a real fellowship. Their impressions of His teaching and His ideals instead of growing fainter with the passing of the years grew more intense and vivid.

(B) Again, after the passing of Jesus, the disciples became endued with immense spiritual power; their faith, which before had often been hesitant and flickering, burnt with a strong and steady flame; their enthusiasm was unbounded. After the first shock of the passing of their Master was over, they were swept along on a tidal wave of confidence and expectancy. They were not a company of disappointed and dispirited followers of a dead or absent Teacher, as must have been the case if they had felt any real separation from their Leader. Their story is a story of men and women in actual contact with their Leader, responding to the magic spell of a living personality. There is something in all this which cannot be explained by the usual phenomena of a great movement. How is it to be explained? Although strongly tinged with the element of the mysterious and unusual, the readiest explanation (and the one least surrounded with difficulties) is, that the conviction which filled the mind and heart of Jesus of His continued presence with and ministry to His disciples, was absolutely realized in fact: that although He had passed from the external and visible world, He was, as He had promised, manifested in the soul of the disciple who loved Him and tried to live in loyal obedience to His teaching and ideals.

If it was a delusion, then it was a delusion which accomplished exactly what the reality was designed to accomplish, and that is not usually the way with delusions.

As we pass in review the literature of the New Testament: in the Gospel narrative, in the story of the apostolic propaganda, in the letters of teaching and exhortation which passed from apostle to Church or individual—we find this emerging, that the presence of Christ with and in the individual disciple was believed in as a fact of experience, as firmly as anything recorded in the story of the wonderful life of the Master. And further, the power of the Gospel over the hearts and in the lives of the disciples was by every one attributed to the indwelling Christ. It was in fact the "Christ in us" to which they referred their "manner of life," and their hope for the future.

Held in the absolute and simple way in which they held it it may seem to be mysterious to us beyond our comprehension. But, that a factor in Religion is mysterious, does not, as has been pointed out, prove it to be irrational or impossible. As to the reality of that in which the early disciples believed we have to judge by the probabilities of the case and the evidence in its favour, and judged on that basis we have to admit it.

It is the absolute justification of the principle of the New Apologetic. In returning to it, and taking it as the centre of gravity of our thought and faith, we are returning to the outstanding fact in the history of the first century, and appropriating for ourselves the motive force of its life. We ask ourselves, is there anything, has anything happened to render that principle invalid and the force inoperative, along the centuries since the first? We can find nothing either in the promise of His presence as given by Jesus, or in history to justify any supposition of the kind.

If the promise was good for the disciple of the first century, why should it not be good for the disciple of the twentieth? If He continued to be the Teacher and Guide of the disciples of those early days, and individual contact with Him the mainspring of their life of Faith—why should it be different for us?

There is nothing to suggest that Jesus intended to limit this personal relation in the individual experience to the earliest of His disciples. It is logically inevitable that whatever we recognize to have been the case with them is equally true, at any rate in possibility, for us. So we arrive at the conclusion, which is strange and startling to us only because we have lacked the logical imagination to perceive it, that for the humblest disciple to-day there is possible the direct and personal contact with Christ, with all its consequent enlightenment and power, which was actual in the apostolic days. And we may go a step further and say, that enlightenment and power, a faith and life illuminated and energized by the Christ, are always the result of personal contact with Him in the experience of every human soul that possesses them; and without it they cannot exist.

The average man thinks of Jesus Christ as one far removed from the actualities of his life, separated by a wide gulf of nearly twenty long centuries from him ; a man in a book. If only we had lived in the days when He lived and taught in Galilee, if we could have seen Him with our eyes, and heard His voice with our ears, and felt the magic spell of His personal presence ; how we would have responded to His appeal ! Or if we had lived in that marvellous first century, and felt in ourselves the magnetic forces, and shared in the mysterious influences of the unseen presence of the Christ, which transformed men and women of common mould into the saints and heroes who have won the homage of following ages, we too would have been even as they were. But our trouble is that the Christ who was so real and near to them is vague and remote to us. What the average man to-day needs to realize is that it is his lack of faith and spiritual perception, or perhaps his lack of interest, that is the trouble ; that now as ever in the days of old the Christ will come to the lowly soul, to him who will throw open the door of his heart, and make his abode with Him.

And the witness of history in the first century is reiterated in all the subsequent centuries. It is quite clear that whenever in any age or place, in the lives of individuals or in the experience of the Church, there has been a return to this living fellowship with the Christ present in the heart, there has always been a flood tide of faith and power; and the phenomena of the first century have, in their essential characteristics, been repeated, though the forms in which they have been embodied may have been different according to varying circumstances and conditions.

We find it so in the story of St. Francis of Assisi, of John Wesley, of Charles Haddon Spurgeon, in the story of the Reformation, and of the Evangelical Revival of the eighteenth century, in the story of modern missions, or of the Salvation Army.

What has been before can be again, and will be, and is, as the necessary condition is fulfilled. The joy, the courage, the enthusiasm, the power, the faith which has transformed and transfigured human life may be ours any day, if we will open our hearts to the Christ and allow Him to do His redeeming work within us.

The witness of history will find its joyful corroboration in the life and experience of the humblest and most insignificant among us.

SOME OBJECTIONS TO THE NEW APOLOGETIC

CHAPTER VII

SOME OBJECTIONS TO THE NEW APOLOGETIC

THE position taken up in the preceding chapters raises some important questions which have to be faced and answered. The modern point of view, which, after all, is only a reversion to that of Jesus and of the New Testament, affects the whole range of Christian Theology. It is obviously beyond the scope of these papers to prosecute an elaborate and detailed analysis of the effect of the new standpoint on the doctrine and practice of the Christian Church. It involves in some respects a complete reversal of old methods of proving the truth of religion and justifying one's Christian Faith. More and more the tendency is to shift the fortress of apologetic to this new ground, and to intrench religious certitude behind the defensive rampart of the individual spiritual experience.

But having laid down new lines of defence it is well that we should go over them to search for any possible weak places at which hostile criticism may penetrate the lines, and effect the discomfiture of Faith.

And the New Apologetic has not long to wait before being assailed by objections, urged with equal vigour, from two opposite camps of criticism—from the side of the older orthodoxy which bases the claims and defence of the Faith on the ground of external authority, and from the side of the current scepticism which is agnostic toward everything that lies outside the region of physical phenomena or goes beyond the lowest common measure of what is universally demonstrated; an agnosticism which finds truth only in the universal experience and refuses to regard as valid any truth which lies within the purely personal experience.

Both of these sources of criticism, Authority and scientific Agnosticism, are really the expression of the same fundamental point of view that nothing is valid in the nature of Truth which cannot be referred to the universal experience. It is a curious example of the meeting of extremes.

Here are some of the main objections urged against the principle that the ultimate proof of religious Truth lies in the spiritual experience of the individual. It is said that Religion becomes a merely personal affair, limited in range and narrow in scope. It reduces Faith to the level of him who holds it, a personal idiosyncrasy as little and ignorant, as unreliable and unstable as may be the individuality of the man himself. It robs faith of the Divine sanction, it becomes an entirely human product, it ceases to be the gift of God, the revelation of God to man, it becomes nothing more than the product of the human consciousness, undisciplined by the Divine guidance, it springs from the earth, and is of the earth earthy.

Again, it is urged that a Faith based on the spiritual experiences of the individual leads to an attitude of spiritual isolation, justifies an extreme and irrational individualism and ends in spiritual anarchy ; that it destroys the solidarity of Religion ; religious fellowship is impossible, historic continuity of the Faith is impossible, the Church is impossible. You can have no Religion in any large sense binding human souls together in a living unity of faith, you can only have a jumble of unrelated religious idiosyncrasies ; Religion becomes a thing of shreds and patches.

These are some of the chief objections brought against the principle upon which the modern Apologetic is based. They are sufficiently serious to demand our careful consideration.

As we examine them we find that they fall into two divisions.

1. Those which spring out of a suspicion of the competency of the individual to arrive at an adequate Faith.

2. Those which arise out of a failure to recognize the elements which govern the mutual relations of the individual and the society.

Let us deal with them in this order—

1. Objections based on the incompetency of the individual for the attainment of a satisfying and satisfactory Faith.

(*a*) Let us say at once that one must accept freely the criticism that a Religion based on personal experience does make Religion a personal affair. And our contention is just this, that Religion is at root properly a personal affair; it springs out of the individual consciousness, it is not, and cannot be, a universal fact until it has become established as an individual experience. Religion in the larger inclusiveness of the term is only possible by being, in the first instance, an individual and inward vision.

To use a logical phrase its connotation is the result of the fusing together of its denotation in single and separate cases.

When the word is used to express the sum of the Faith professed by a community or Society its content is made up of the elements which emerge out of the spiritual experience of the individuals of the Society, blended into a harmonious unity. The wider sense of the word always presupposes the coming together and fusing of religion in the narrower sense. It is this personal religion, based on the inward experiences of the individual which comes first in the logical order, and which lies at the base of Religion in the wider and universal sense.

Fundamentally, then, Religion is an individual affair. When a man says "I believe," and says it with the earnestness and intensity of a real Faith, he is thinking of the things which he holds, not as held in common with others, but as things which he has seen with his own spiritual vision, and which have entered into his own experience, which have taken shape and form in his own meditations upon the facts of life.

And what is more, he can only say it, with any real conviction, of those things.

One source of the weakness of Religion in the wider sense—its frequent failure to appeal to the conscience—is, that men are so ready to affix their "I believe" to a Faith, a large phase of which lies entirely outside their own experience; in regard to such they can have no real conviction, only, at best, an opinion—and opinion counts for little or nothing in matters of Faith, it must be rooted in conviction. To be vital and forceful, Faith must have been generated in the spiritual laboratory of the individual soul.

One of the things that our age needs most to realize is just this fact embodied in the criticism intended to be hostile, that Religion, to be of any real value to the man himself, must be a personal affair, and he can only participate in the wider Religion of the Society, effectually to himself or to It, as he has won his own Faith out of the spiritual experience of his own soul.

(*b*) And this personal religion must be limited in range and narrow in scope, i.e. as limited and narrow as the personal experience and outlook. You cannot "believe," in the sense of faith, that of which you have had no experience. We accept the criticism as the witness of reality and the standard of value.

Say if you will that the resulting creed will include fewer articles, and be, logically, more imperfect. But the reply is obvious. What we lose in range we gain in intensity; what we lose in quantity we gain in quality; what we lose in logical perfection we gain in spiritual power. It is better to believe in a few things with a passionate intensity born of a real contact with facts, than to believe many things mechanically, which we accept from some Authority external to ourselves. It is better to have a kingdom of Faith which our own sword can defend than a far wider empire of creed with an undefendable border, open to the incursion of any and every foe to Faith.

(*c*) A similar answer can be made to the objection that a Faith springing out of the individual experience will be marked and marred by all the weaknesses, the defects, the prejudices of the individual. This again has to be freely admitted. We accept the inevitable limitation. But we are willing to have a Faith so marred, if it be alive with personal intensity, rather than a Faith which, however perfect in its purity and completeness, lacks the vitality and power which the personality of the man who has won it for himself can alone give to it. An imperfect

Faith penetrated with the manhood of the believer, will be far more powerful in his life as an uplifting and redeeming force, than a perfect Faith received on authority from some external source and lacking the driving power which can only be generated from within.

And then, when all is said, we have to recognize that there is no such thing as a perfect Faith, absolutely pure, marred by no human weakness or prejudice. We are asked to relinquish the Faith which has been wrought out of our own personal experience because it must be narrowed by our own limitations, marred by the flaws of our own mind and heart; and to accept in its place some other which comes to us guaranteed by the sanction of some weighty Authority.

"How should you," we are asked, "cling to your own imperfect and foolish thought, when there is provided for you the dicta of synod and council, of Church and Pope, into which all the wisdom of scholar and saint, all the ripe experience of antiquity have been concentrated?"

But when we turn to examine the Faith that is so given we find, in every case, that it also is marked and marred by human limitations and weakness and prejudice; its ideas, not seldom, conflicting; its very terms with double meanings and strange ambiguities, so that the framers of it fall out in their interpretations.

Is it the Faith of the Roman Church we are asked to accept? We find it deeply scarred with all the human characteristics of temper and feeling, of intellectual bias and ecclesiastical prejudice. In its making, political considerations have not seldom largely entered; its articles have been forced through by chicanery where argument failed—and the whole presented often at the sword's point, by the carnal weapons of civil states rather than by the earnest persuasion of the spirit, and enforced with thumbscrew and rack.

Or is it the Protestant confession which

claims our allegiance? In every variant of it you find evident traces of the personal weakness, the idiosyncrasies, the intellectual bias, the spiritual temper of the men who framed it. Genevan and Lutheran, Anglican and British Nonconformist, all have wrought into their creeds the temperament, the educational bias, the national and race characteristics of the men who framed them.

Such a thing as a Faith void of the human element is non-existent, and in the nature of the case impossible. The power which the ancient creeds have in their time possessed over the hearts of men has sprung from their human content. In so far as they have corresponded to what men have found in their own experience they have exercised their sway and fulfilled their purpose. If the common Faith of the Society is not so corroborated it can be in the heart of the individual nothing but a fetish.

And why should we be afraid to trust our own mind and heart in matters of Faith?

Imperfect and limited, the result, at the best, will be But has there not been made to us the promise of the Spirit Who should dwell in us, and lead all who in earnestness and sincerity yield themselves to Him, into all Truth ? That promise was made not to the Church as a body, not to the writers of the New Testament as the future authors of an infallible Canon of Scripture, but it was given to the individual disciples, and it was intended to hold good for all who in future ages should seek to be faithful disciples of Jesus—for the humblest, and simplest, and most insignificant of them That promise is itself the witness to the intention of the Christ that each disciple should for himself, and out of his own experience, construct the fabric of his Faith. We are all of us liable to err, as we are human —Pope and Cardinal, Bishop and Priest and Layman, but that liability is modified and its danger guarded against for the sincere disciple by the guidance of the Spirit of God Himself, Who will, if we trust and follow Him, in spite of all our weakness and limitations, lead us to a satisfying and satisfactory and effective Faith.

(*d*) The presence of the guiding Spirit of God in the heart and mind of the disciple meets, too, the objection, that if the Faith is the product of the individual experience wrought upon by mind and heart, it is no longer a revelation from God, and has no Divine sanction.

If we believe in the real presence of the Spirit of God abiding in the disciple, then surely the gradual emergence of faith out of experience in which God is at work, is as much a revelation of God and bears the Divine sanction as though it were written in characters of fire across the sky; or at least as though it came to us from some ecclesiastical Authority. The creed of the Church is as much a human product, as much of the earth earthy as the Faith won for himself by the individual. God speaks to each man of us, as truly in our own thought and experience as in the written word of Scripture or in the dicta of Council and Church.

Jesus has taught us to believe that God writes His law upon our hearts, that the Father speaks to His child.

2. And now we come to the objections to the New Apologetic, based on the idea of the Solidarity of Religion, which it is supposed to violate. "Although Religion may be a personal affair," it is said, "it is also essentially a bond of union, linking men together in a community or fellowship."

The element of association is just as necessary to the vitality and power of Religion as is the element of individuality. If the personal factor is allowed to dominate to the extent of destroying the solidarity of Faith, then Religion loses its expansive power, and becomes simply a spiritual anarchy.

All these objections, however they may be expressed, amount to the same thing, and arise out of a failure to recognize the elements which govern the mutual relation of the individual and the Society.

The individual and the Community have been, in popular Sociology, dragged into the position of opposed and conflicting entities. That is a false position because, first, there is no opposition, no conflict between them; and secondly, the Community is not an entity at all, i.e. as apart from the individual, and is at root nothing more than a relation. An important and essential relation, but a relation after all. The Community is simply a realized function of the individual in active and healthy operation. The social bond is a phase of individuality. If there were no individuals there could be no Society. While the reverse is not true, yet without the Society the individual would be atrophied on one side of his being; a legitimate and natural function of individuality would find no sphere for activity.

The Society exists for the individual. That is the broad ground which has to be taken in the last analysis. Whatever the claims and authority of the Society may be, they are only good for (they may be tested and approved by) their reactive influence upon individual life ; in so far as that is perfected and fulfilled by them.

The Society has a twofold function—Defensive and Progressive. Defensive, i.e. it defends the individual, in the exercise of his legitimate functions, against the illegitimate activities of conflicting individuality : it maintains the proper balance of the individual life ; and Progressive, i.e. it creates a condition and relation in which individuality may, properly safeguarded, attain its highest fulfilment. It is always the individual first and last that stands behind and is the reason for the existence of the Community.

The life and power of the Community, of the Race, depend upon the freedom and efficiency of the individual. The history of the Race witnesses to the universality of this law. The communities in which the individual has been enslaved, his life cramped and narrowed, in which he has been sacrificed to the Society, have always ended prematurely, in disaster and ruin. Those, on the other hand, which, while keeping him within his legitimate activities, have left the individual the fullest freedom and encouraged his development, have endured longest and have accomplished the finest results in the achievement of human destiny. If Nature seems careless of the single life and careful of the type, yet her care for the type is only another form of her larger ministry to individual perfection. The great quest of the world's builders of Society to-day is, to find that form of the common life, that expression of the Social bond in which the single life may, through freedom, find room for its finest and fullest development.

Carry all this over into the region of Religion and the Christian Faith, and it meets the objections urged against the New Apologetic as being detrimental to the solidarity of

Religion, and the bond of the Fellowship of the Christian Church.

Jesus came primarily to save the individual, rather than to build up a Church. The Church exists for the individual ; and the individual for the Church only to make its reactive influence on the individual more effective and helpful. Jesus came to make men good, to purify and redeem, to release the Divine potentiality of the human soul ; and the Church exists as a means to that end. It is only by the culture and development of the Faith of the individual, won out of his own experience, that the Church can have any power or vitality at all.

So far from the Faith of the inward vision being in opposition to the interest of the common Faith, the latter is fed by the former and depends upon it for very existence. In proportion as the inward vision fades, the common Faith becomes only a sepulchre. We must not allow a false opposition to be set up between them.

What is the common Faith, the Church's doctrine, the Communion of Saints, the historic Unity, the Continuity of the Faith? What is it all but the blending together in a harmonious unity, the greatest common measure, of the individual experience? There can only be real Union, real Fellowship, persistent Continuity, in that which is common to all, in the things which are equally true for the individual as for the Society.

Human experience has much in common; life is, in its main elements, much alike. Diverse in its more superficial aspects, as we get deep down to the springs of being we find ourselves approaching one another, and it is out of all that is common to all in the deeper regions that the common Faith emerges; a Faith that binds the individual disciples in the Fellowship of the Church, and persists through the ages. The historic Continuity of the Faith rests, not on the unbroken continuance of any external organization, but upon the persistence of the type, of the human element, amidst all the changes and variety of external conditions.

Behind and at the foundation of all Religion lies the fact of the soul's vision of the Eternal. The Church, the historic Faith, the Communion of Saints, the vital power and permanence of Religion—all rest ultimately on the reality, and intensity, and clarity of that vision ; on the things that eye hath not seen, nor ear heard, but which the Spirit reveals to the soul in the silence of the secret and inner shrine of the individual life. *There* is the central source and spring of Religion, and there ultimately all its problems must find their final solution.

THE ESSENTIAL AND THE ACCIDENTAL IN THE CHRISTIAN FAITH

CHAPTER VIII

THE ESSENTIAL AND THE ACCIDENTAL IN THE CHRISTIAN FAITH

ONE of the easiest things in the world is to demolish an opponent's case if he will only allow us to state it for him. By ignoring the points in his argument for which we have no answer, by giving prominence to the premises which are obviously weak, by over-emphasis of this particular and under-statement of that, there is no case, no theory, no presentation of Truth, which cannot be made to look absurd and be laughed out of court as absolutely ridiculous.

There are some people who have a special faculty for this kind of thing. They will never attempt to discuss any question fairly and squarely, but will endeavour to re-state the question in terms which, eliminating the strong points and emphasizing the weak, will make its refutation quite easy.

This is a favourite method with many who take upon themselves to "expose," as they say, Christianity. Probably the large majority of them have never had a close personal experience of Christianity. And it is impossible to understand Christianity unless it has been related to one's personal experience. The man who simply views it and deals with it as something external to himself, as something outside his experience, is not in a position to assert either the truth or otherwise of Christianity.

In most cases, charity urges us to believe that there is no deliberate attempt to misrepresent; there is only sheer ignorance of the essential elements of the Christian Faith.

It is necessary, if we are to discuss a matter fairly, that we should acquaint ourselves with the most exact, logical, scholarly and scientific statement of the case we are contesting. We should know all the best that can be said in its favour, and said in the best way. It would be absurd, for example, in discussing questions of physical science, to argue on the basis of the science of a hundred years ago. That would be a vain beating of the air, a "ploughing of the sand."

It is exactly the same in the science of Christian Theology. The man who thinks he is exposing Christianity by arguing on the basis of the Theology of a hundred years ago is hardly worth listening to.

One interesting phase of the movements of the modern religious mind is the very general interest in, and study of, the great Eastern Religions, and of Buddhism in particular.

That is all to the good. We are beginning to break down the limitations which have been presumptuously cast around the conception of the operation of God's truth-giving Spirit: to understand that not in Palestine only, but in all the world and among all peoples, God has been revealing Himself to the hearts of men. A considerable number of writers who have made a close study of Buddhism, and drunk deeply of its spirit, have set themselves the happy task of winning from the Western mind a juster estimate of the Eastern Faith.

But in comparing Buddhism with Christianity, if it is necessary to compare, why should it be necessary, as is often done, to take the crudest, least scientific, the least intelligent statement of the Christian Faith, and put it by the side of the purest, most highly-cultured and idealized forms of Buddhism? That is hardly fair, to say nothing else. It is easy to depreciate Christianity and to exalt Buddhism on those terms.

There is only mischief done to Truth in any sphere, either of physical Science, economics, history, medicine, or theology, by the cheap discussion of questions: when those who are discussing know little or nothing of the latest and most exact conclusions on the matter at issue, and when they have only picked up their information from a hurried and superficial reading of some out-of-date text-book.

In no case is this more true than in regard to the Christian Faith.

A good deal of the destructive criticism urged against Christianity to-day does not apply to the Christian Faith at all, but affects only the forms in which the Faith has, from time to time, been stated. Many of these forms have been outgrown and discarded years ago by its exponents. It is easy to appear to demolish Christianity if one takes the crudest forms in which it has been stated (forms which were adequate to and harmonious with the limits of knowledge of the time at which they were framed) and then proceeds to test those forms by the standard of the vastly widened limits of knowledge to-day. It is very necessary that we should clearly understand that what is attacked, and often demolished, is not the Gospel of Christ, but the forms in which that Gospel has been stated. Giving those who lead the attack credit for honesty of purpose, the very selection of those creeds and outworn forms shows their ignorance of the real issues involved in the Christian Faith, and their own incompetence to deal with the subject.

In estimating the truth and value of the Gospel of Jesus we need, as far as possible, to distinguish clearly between what is essential to it and what is non-essential. It is necessary to get a clear conception of the teaching of the facts, which constitute the Gospel, and to separate and hold it apart from whatever has, subsequently to its deliverance by Jesus, been added to it or associated with it by His followers. It is plain to the student of the history of the Faith that certain elements have been associated with Christ's message by the Church in the progress of the centuries, which, however close their relation to it, are by no means necessary to the message itself, and can be accepted or rejected without affecting its truth or lessening its value.

If we were to review the attacks that have been made upon Christianity we should find that in the large majority of cases, and in every case in which those attacks have been successful, they have been urged against these non-essential elements. It may be said that there is hardly anyone who questions the truth or value of the Gospel of Jesus pure and simple.

Let us illustrate this distinction between the message of Jesus and the things that have been added to it, by a few examples.

1 For hundreds of years in the history of the Christian Church, the doctrine of Transubstantiation was regarded as part and parcel of the Christian Faith. Its denial would have been sufficient to secure the excommunication from the Church of the man who had the temerity to reject it. To hold that doctrine was regarded as essential to

the Christian Faith, its rejection was tantamount, in the eyes of the Church, to a rejection of the Faith. It stood, in the Theology of the Church, for the one and only effective process whereby the grace and promises, the gifts and powers of the Gospel could be bestowed upon the individual. It was, and is to-day, the very foundation of the spiritual supremacy possessed by the Church holding it. It is the pivot around which the faith and doctrine, the organization and ritual of the Church move.

Yet is there one of the millions of Protestant Christians in Western Christendom who would imagine that the rejection of the doctrine of Transubstantiation involves the rejection of the Gospel of Jesus? We now recognize it as something which, though for centuries regarded as part and parcel of the Gospel, forms no essential part of the message of Jesus; and indeed, for us, its rejection only serves to bring us into closer touch with and clearer perception of the Gospel.

This will be, for most of us, an extreme case, but it is suggested that the principle involved in this extreme example applies all the way through, viz., that we have to distinguish between what is of the essence of the Faith, and what has been associated with it by others.

Let us illustrate further :—

2. There are the doctrines of " The Church," and " The Sacraments of the Church." That is, associated with the Christian Faith, the idea is widely held that unless a man is admitted to the Church by certain priestly authority and participates in certain sacramental rites he cannot, in any real and effective sense, be a disciple of Christ. Take Christendom throughout, and for the large majority of Christians the doctrines of " the Church " and the " sacraments " are bound up with the Christian Faith. If there is any authority in majorities, any infallibility attaching to a predominant consensus of opinion, then these doctrines form an integral part of the Gospel. But, on the other hand,

there are myriads of men and women who unhesitatingly reject them, and who not only fail to see in their rejection any denial of the Gospel, but also emphatically regard them as something unwarrantably associated with the message of Jesus; such rejection, they hold, brings the soul into closer and more intimate relation with Jesus, and makes His redeeming power more effective in the heart and life.

3. Now let us proceed further along the same line, and apply our principle to the doctrines of the Church which are generally accepted, not by one or two sections only of the Church, but by nearly all of them; catholic doctrines in almost the most absolute sense of the term—such for example as the doctrines of the Incarnation, of the Atonement, of the Trinity; and all the various and subtle modifications of them.

These, or the particular statement of them which we accept, are the way in which we have tried to express, or accept as expressing, the facts and truths we have realized in our experience of the Gospel as we have related it to our personal needs ; the interpretation of the Gospel in the terms of our own experience. The facts and truths are in the Gospel ; the statement of them in terms of experience (i.e. as doctrines) is our own. We may have apprehended them imperfectly. Our experience, at the widest, is partial and one-sided, making our interpretation of them partial and inadequate. The fact is always greater, the truth fuller, than our doctrinal statement of it can possibly be.

It is entirely conceivable that any one may reject the interpretation of the facts and truths proclaimed by Jesus given by any other one, and yet believe in the facts and accept the truths and give them an interpretation which, according better with the individual experience, appeals with greater force to the individual mind and heart.

If this be granted it follows inevitably that the Gospel of Jesus is separate from the doctrines, the rites, the organization of the Church. It soars far above and beyond them. They are of value in proportion as they interpret truly, for the individual, the surpassing Gospel, and are penetrated by its spirit and genius. They are alive, powerful, effective for the individual, the Church, or the Age as they bring the Christ with His message of redeeming love and power into the mind and heart and life of individual, Church, or civilization. But they are no more than the media by which the Gospel is applied to the heart of man, they are no more than channels along which the water of the river of life flows to the thirsty soul. They are not the river itself, the vivifying water. Sometimes the river changes its channel to accord with the changing conditions, and the old channels dry up and are useless save as historical landmarks; but the main thing is that the life-giving water should reach the soil of the human soul and make it to blossom as the garden of the Lord.

Half the troubles about belief, half the difficulty of faith, half the doubts of men arise from the simple cause that they do not distinguish between the facts and truths of the Gospel as Jesus stated them, and the interpretations, the doctrines, the rites, which men have associated with them. We must recognize, for our own security of faith, that criticism of doctrine and the modification or even rejection of any doctrine, however widely held, do not involve rejection of the Gospel, do not affect the truth of the message of which the rejected doctrine is the, to us, inadequate statement; such message will, if we are sincere and in earnest, be made true to us by some other channel of expression.

So, then, in view of the popular attacks on Christianity, attacks which are plausible enough if we allow its opponents to state its case; he who would come to a fair judgment on the matter must be aware of the distinction between the message of Jesus as

He delivered it, and the ideas, doctrines, practices which, being associated with it, have by long and general acceptance so grown into it as to seem of its essence.

Sometimes the doctrine attacked does not receive our consent. Then hostile criticism leaves us untouched as regards our hold on the Christian Faith.

But it may happen that the criticism is urged, and successfully urged, against some form of faith's expression which has been valid for us; and, however reluctantly, we feel ourselves driven in sincerity to relinquish an interpretation of the Gospel which has, through the long years, satisfied both mind and heart. What is to happen then? Is our faith in Jesus and our hold upon His Gospel to slacken and pass, and the music of His Glad Tidings to turn to discord, because we find that our understanding of such has been imperfect?

Let us rather recognize that since our interpretation has been inadequate and unsound, the plain thing before us is to seek for some interpretation of the Gospel which shall accord with the changed conditions, the new point of view, and make it for us still the power of God for the Salvation of our souls.

Thus we are led to the all-important conclusion that the best exponent of the Gospel of Jesus is Jesus Himself, and he who would learn what Truth in Jesus really is must go for his instruction most to the fountain head, must yield himself to the Divine Teacher who uttered the words of life and love and power to the peasants of Galilee nineteen hundred years ago, and Who will not less clearly or directly declare the Truth to sincere and earnest hearts to-day. He, too, will give us the true doctrine, the right interpretation, in the terms of our own personal experience, of the message that is of universal application. Jesus Himself is our Teacher to-day as much as He was the Teacher of the Twelve who gathered about Him and lived in closest communion with Him in the three years of marvellous earthly ministry.

It is well that we should listen and try to understand as others tell us what they have found in Christ, that we should listen sympathetically, and for our own instruction, as others interpret the Gospel in terms of their experience. It is right and good for us that we should sit at the feet of the great thinkers and saints who expound the message in the light of human nature and human needs, and weave their conclusions into creed and doctrine and theology. There is nothing more shallow, more ignorant, than the scoff so often cast at the doctrines and theology of the Church. The man who ignores or holds cheaply the rich treasure of human experience, the revelation of the human heart in its agonizing after Truth and God which these doctrines and creeds contain, is lacking in reverence for human nature and looks at life in a perverse and distorted perspective.

But above all the thought of saint and

scholar stands the Christ. At the best their thoughts and systems are but broken lights of Him.

It is not enough that we should be content with a reflected knowledge of Jesus.

After all that man can say to us has been said, we must go into the secret and lonely place where the voice of the Christ alone is heard. We must correct all our thoughts, all the teachings of the wise and holy, by the teaching of Him who is wiser and holier than all. We must live in the atmosphere of Christ, we must yield ourselves to the influence of His Spirit present with every sincere disciple, so that we may be prepared by Him to receive and understand and be able to apply His teaching to our own spiritual necessities.

We must see the Christ through our own eyes, if we are ever to see Him as He was and is.

If, and whenever, we are in doubt about the Christian Faith, if we are wearied and perplexed with the thoughts and theories of men about the Christ and His Gospel, it will be well for us to close the books of doctrine, to leave the discussion of creeds, to cease to follow the complexities of theological science, especially to turn from the noisy criticism of a certain type of journalism, cheap, irreverent and self-assertive, and in quiet meditation upon the words and deeds of the great Teacher, in rapt communion with His Spirit, to listen again to the great Gospel of Galilean days.

As has been said above, it is an interesting fact that nearly the whole weight of hostile criticism has been thrown against, not the Gospel, but the things that have been associated with it. When the critic stands face to face with the Christ he is silent. Criticism is hushed and disarmed. When the opponent of the doctrines and forms in which the Christian Faith has been expressed pushes his way into the presence of the Christ Himself, he adopts the reverent attitude, and in silence bows to adore, and leaves the Sacred Presence to take up, if he does take up again, his criticism of the Externals of the Faith with a chastened and subdued spirit.

Jesus can take care of Himself. When the human heart comes into touch with Him, foe is transformed to friend—Love and Purity incarnated in the Christ still exercise their ancient spell. In the serene atmosphere of communion and fellowship with Him all the noise of the battlefield of creed and criticism dies away, the obscurities created by imperfect human thought and reasoning in theology and philosophy become translucent, and as we look into His Face, and listen to His words, we realize that it was no empty boast when He said, "I, if I be lifted up, will draw all men unto Myself."

THE INCREASE OF KNOWLEDGE AND THE GROWTH OF FAITH

CHAPTER IX

THE INCREASE OF KNOWLEDGE AND THE GROWTH OF FAITH

ONE of the most striking features in the story of modern times is the wonderful enlargement in the store of human knowledge. An advance has been made, so rapid and wide-reaching as to be almost bewildering. It has been an age of discovery, undreamed of continents in the world of knowledge have been opened up.

The most startling results have, perhaps, been achieved in the realms of physical science. But though the results in that direction have been more dazzling and have appealed to the popular taste for the marvellous, the march of the explorer has not been confined to that region. In all directions the horizon of "the known" has been immensely widened.

And not only in each separate science has knowledge been increased. Advance in one direction has given the impulse for advance all round; discovery in one branch of inquiry has suggested discovery in another. We have had impressed upon us the fact of the unity of all knowledge. Each new fact revealed to us is but the revelation from a new point of view of the one Eternal Fact at the centre of all things which manifests itself to us in varying forms and along various channels. There is one "divine event," one "increasing purpose," to the unfolding of which the whole creation is slowly but surely moving.

For the man who is in earnest about his Faith this increase of knowledge raises, and will raise even more insistently in the future, an important question which cannot be evaded. He must ask himself, "What ought my attitude to be towards this ever-growing accumulation of new facts ? "

The advance in knowledge cannot leave one's religious Faith untouched and unaffected. Faith must at least keep in line with knowledge, to lag behind is disastrous. We cannot shut Religion and Faith off from knowledge, and say " Whatever happens, whatever new facts are brought to light, nothing shall make any difference to my religious beliefs." Faith may be defined as the spiritual interpretation of the facts of the world and human life. If known facts are modified, or new facts are discovered, inevitably the question is raised :—what effect does the modification or the discovery have upon that spiritual interpretation ?

Finding ourselves in the possession of an immense store of new knowledge, there are two or three courses open to us. We may take up an attitude of no compromise. We may say to ourselves. " My religious Faith is altogether above and beyond any facts of mere human knowledge. Religion has nothing to do with physical science, or history, or economics, or sociology, and I will steadfastly ignore all new facts, as far as my Religion is concerned, and go on believing the same things and expressing my Faith in exactly the same forms as before."

We should very soon find that attitude to be impossible unless we were content to live in an unreal world. We should never be able to rest content with a Religion in flat contradiction to the facts of life which we found about us every day. We should soon lose all respect for Religion. It would degenerate into the merest superstition. The very necessities of thought would drive us to follow some other line. Then we have to choose between two alternatives :—

1. To cling to the old forms of Faith and deny the new facts ; to say, " My Faith is the touchstone by which the truth of everything, even of physical and historical facts, must be

tested. If what claims to be a new fact does not square with my religious beliefs it is thereby proved false."

This attitude is by no means uncommon. It was, for example, very largely adopted by religious people in the days when Charles Darwin propounded his theory of Evolution. "Your new facts, and your theory," they said, "do not agree with my Faith built up on the opening chapters of the Book of Genesis, they do not harmonize with my belief about the way God acts in the world, therefore your facts must be false, and your theory impious and blasphemous." Or again; a certain view of Scripture is maintained, a belief in the absolute and equal infallibility of all its parts, and all the results of Biblical criticism, all the labours of devout scholarship, are contemptuously swept on one side, because they conflict with the mechanical belief in the verbal inspiration of the Bible.

2. The alternative to this attitude is to accept the new facts if the proof of them

is sufficient and satisfactory, and then to modify, as far as is necessary, the forms in which our religious faith expresses itself, so that faith and knowledge may, as far as possible, be in accord.

The special difficulties of either position are these :—

1. If we adopt the former attitude, then the man of Science charges us with being blind and narrow, unreasonable and bigoted, shutting our eyes to everything we cannot explain, making prejudice and ignorance the test of truth, meeting argument and reason by stupidly reiterating "No." And of course he treats this blind denial of his facts with undisguised contempt, he himself is estranged from a Faith which takes up such an attitude, and a wide breach, a deep hostility, is created between Religion and Science.

2. But if we adopt the latter alternative, then we have to meet the cries of "heretic," "blasphemous," "infidel," from many on

our own side; we are excommunicated from fellowship, or at least, regarded with deep suspicion as traitors to the Faith. In addition we have to meet, not seldom, the sneers of a certain type of scientist who says, with a curious lack of logical consistency, "What a strange religion yours must be, how elastic and conveniently adaptable. To-day you base your Faith on one set of facts, and to-morrow, when they are disproved, you shift on to new ground and believe as comfortably as ever. Religion that is one thing to-day and another thing to-morrow cannot be worth anything at any time." He would have us throw Faith overboard altogether and become at least agnostic.

This is the difficulty which the average man finds confronting him. What is he to do? Do the new facts, which are undeniable, necessitate his repudiation of Faith? Or is he to cling blindly to the old facts in face of all the evidence, because the new will involve a modification in the forms of belief in which his Faith has formerly been expressed? Or is it possible to modify his belief so as to accord with the new knowledge, and yet be true to himself; to find a new form for the old Faith which shall embody all that is proved in the new, and yet retain all that was essential in the old?

Let us try to find a way out of the difficulty, saying at once that this last course is, in spite of the sneers of the sceptic, or the denunciation of the rigidly orthodox, the true, logical, and honest course to follow.

Let us go back for a moment to our definition of Faith, as the spiritual interpretation of the facts of the world and of human life. Our religious Faith is the sum of our perception of the spiritual significance of those facts.

If that is a valid definition of Faith, then two things follow:—

First, that for faith at any rate, it is not the fact on its external side that matters, but the spiritual significance of it. The fact is the husk, its relation to the spiritual order is the kernel. Second, we can at no time go beyond the facts of experience, i.e. experience of the external world, or of the inner world of thought and feeling.

The facts are the symbols in which the truth is expressed; the symbol must never be more precious than the truth, the one must never be allowed to obscure the other. And yet we have to learn; the truth has to be communicated, embodied in some form, and our perception of the Truth will always be dependent on its expression in symbol. Our knowledge of the facts of the world and human life will always be limited, since omniscience is in the nature of the case denied us. At the best and fullest it must be partial. We can never have a complete and perfect knowledge; that belongs to God alone. We can only see a segment of the completed circle. However we view Truth, we only view it at any time from an angle. But we may move from point to point. The angle of vision may widen, and, with widening vision, knowledge increases, new facts come into the line of sight ;—and, as they come, the significance of each has to be added to what we already know, either to confirm the spiritual interpretation of the narrower vision, or to modify it, and so involve a re-adjustment of Faith.

This is the natural view to take. There is nothing in the Bible or in the sayings of Jesus against it. Indeed, this is the attitude which Jesus Himself suggests as proper for His disciples. "I have yet many things to say unto you, but ye cannot bear them now." Some of those "many things" doubtless have still to be revealed to us.

If we are to regard Faith as fixed and final, then of course no modification of our religious belief would be possible. But who says it is fixed? Not Jesus certainly, nor any of His apostles, nor common sense, nor a humble appreciation of our limitations.

What is the final form of Faith? From the very beginning it has been continually growing, and changing its form; which phase of it are we to take as the final and completed form beyond which progress is impossible?

Faith is the spiritual interpretation which at any time may be suggested by the facts which at any time we know. The Faith of to-day is sufficient for to-day, but probably not sufficient for to-morrow. To-morrow there may be wider knowledge, and that ought to mean a larger Faith.

And if Faith is more a present vision than a final creed then the man of science has no room to deny us our right to modify our Faith, or to scoff at its enlargement. He modifies his scientific Faith to take in new facts, why should not we modify our religious Faith for the same purpose.

Another consideration has to be borne in mind. If the forms of our Faith are modified to take in and harmonize with wider knowledge, it does not necessarily involve a denial of the past, it will oftener be found to be a development from the past. The new form which Faith takes on is generally a wider and more affirmative statement of the essential idea embodied in the old form. There is an underlying spiritual unity which links the new with the old.

For example, take the belief in "special creation" such as is described in the Book of Genesis. What is the underlying idea embodied in the Genesis account of the creation? The thought that throbs in and through that wonderful and beautiful narrative is that God is at the back of all creation, the spiritual basis of life. Now the facts that point to an evolutionary process come in, we have to modify the form of our Faith. But though the phraseology may change, though the method is different, it is the same idea of the necessary God behind and in all evolutionary processes. The method of God may be shown to be different from what we imagined, but the fact of God remains unshaken, and some of us think shines more wonderfully, with more dazzling radiance, through the evolutionary process than in special creation.

Half the trouble and bitterness of the changing forms of Faith is the result of blindness to this truth that a modification of the form is mostly a fulfilling, a development, and not a denial of the old.

There is no virtue in change for its own sake. To re-adjust our Faith for the sake of a new sensation is not only silly, but it turns Faith into a mere dilettante trifling with the most sacred and serious issues of life which revenges itself on the manhood of him who indulges in it. But, on the other hand, neither is there any virtue in blindly refusing to recognize the proved facts of the world and human life, or in clinging to beliefs that are out of harmony with those facts. The policy of the ostrich in religious matters is a sign neither of courage, nor of devotion, and it always ends in just the result which one most desires to avoid.

Finally, we need to remember that behind and beneath all our varying forms of Faith, behind all the modifications of belief there stands the reality of God. God is the centre of a spiritual world which lies at the back of the seen and material. The reality of God, and of that world, is the first principle upon which we start to build our Faith. With a firm conviction of that basal fact, and in its light, we can go on to interpret the facts of the world and of human life as they come within our experience. The tides of life's experience may swing us this way or that as they ebb and flow, but fast anchored to God and the reality of the spiritual world, neither ebb nor flow can bring us harm. Every new fact, every varying experience, every advance in knowledge will be the fuller manifestation of the glory of the Lord, flashing up with ever growing radiance above the horizon of human thought; and filling the common world about us with the brightness of His Presence.

"Ah! that is just the point which is, after all, at issue," some one objects, "you have to make that great assumption, to take God for granted." To which we answer both "No," and "Yes." We do not take God for granted in the sense of making a guess, of taking a leap in the dark. We do take Him for granted in the sense in which we take the light for granted at high noontide on a summer's day. The evidence for the reality of God, and of the spiritual world, is as clear and cogent as for any fact of the physical world, though the evidence is of a different order.

The average man, with a true instinct, does not, as a rule, doubt the reality of God. His difficulty begins further along, in relating God to the problems of the common life, in realizing in his own life the God whose existence he accepts, in constructing for himself a working philosophy on that basis.

We may reassure ourselves; there is nothing in the advance of knowledge which has made God less likely, there are a great many things which seem to make Him an inevitable necessity. Let us then begin here, God is the Eternal Reality; then we can go on fearlessly. The world is God's world, He is in all things, all things are the manifestation of His purpose and methods. Every new fact is the revealing of another facet of the life of God, a fuller manifestation of His glory.

So faith ever growing will bring us into fuller perception of and closer touch with the Eternal Love; and every day's life and the wonder-strewn world around will be for us an open page in the radiant romance of the love of God; and the Gospel of Jesus will be the translation of that romance into the language of the common life, and the presence of Jesus in the heart of the earnest and loyal disciple will be the promise and potency of its happy realization for every human soul.

THE CHRISTIAN LIFE

CHAPTER X

THE CHRISTIAN LIFE

THE endeavour has been made in these chapters to state the principle of the New Apologetic of the Christian Faith, and to point out that the surest ground upon which that Faith can rest is not the proclamation of any external Authority, nor the dicta of Church or Council, nor the assertion of priest or preacher, nor the logical and finely constructed arguments of theologian or philosopher, but that which each individual knows in his own experience of what Jesus and His message are to him and do for him, in so far as he gives the Christ the opportunity of being or doing anything. This is the key to most of what is best in modern religious thought. Just as in the realm of physical science the point of view has shifted from that of "special creation" to that of "Evolutionary processes," and the change has affected the entire outlook of scientific inquiry, so in the world of Christian thought the point of view has been moved from external authority to that of the inner witness of the individual experience.

If one wishes to understand the recent movements of religious thought it is quite essential that one should grasp this principle, and perceive its relation to and its effect upon the entire round of Christian Doctrine.

In this closing chapter it is proposed to consider one of the very important corollaries of the principle. A matter which has to do not with abstract questions, but with the practical side of the Christian Faith. Just as the supreme and final proof of the truth of the Gospel of Jesus lies within the individual experience, so the Christian Life, which it is the purpose of Jesus and His message to create, also lies within the experience of the individual disciple. We shall travel over familiar ground and arrive at familiar conclusions, but it is all so important that reiteration is not only pardonable but desirable.

Let us put what has to be said into the form of an answer to the question, What is the Christian Life? That question may seem trite almost to weariness, and the answer so obvious as to be self-evident; still, it is often the trite questions which we ignore, and the self-evident things which we fail to realize.

Suppose this trite question to be put to a company of—say a dozen—average people, what answer should we receive?

Probably each of the twelve answers would be different, at least in some respects, from the rest. But in the larger proportion of them, there would, almost certainly, be one idea at the back of them. The idea that the Christian Life is something external; that it consists mainly in the due performance of certain acts, in conduct which follows certain lines; that it is the acceptance of certain doctrines and the observance of set rites and ceremonies. And some no doubt would add, the association with a certain organized Fellowship. So the Christian Life would be made to consist of that which is concerned with the external side of things; with that which may be tested altogether by an external standard of value.

It is an estimate based on the old point of view. It is in a measure correct because the Christian Life has of course its external side, it must find expression in forms, be embodied in conduct; and the form is some indication of the character of the life of which it is the expression.

But what is ignored in this estimate is the distinction between the Life and the forms in which it expresses itself; between the spirit and the body. It is based on the husk rather than the kernel, on the appearance rather than the thing itself.

"Conduct," Matthew Arnold said, "is three-fourths of life."

That is quite true from one standpoint, and it hardly needs the insight of a philosopher to discover it. But it is quite untrue from another standpoint, with the suggestion that conduct is all that really matters. It is the other one-fourth that lies behind and governs the three-fourths, that determines the character of conduct, and is by far the most important element in life.

And it is exactly the same with the Christian Life. Conduct (the things we say and do, all of life which appears) is three-fourths of discipleship. But it is the one-fourth lying within the heart of the disciple, hidden from the common gaze, known only to the self, and to God, it is that one-fourth that makes conduct, and all that is without, Christian; in *that* lies the secret and essential element of what is called "the Christian Life." What then is that all important one part? It is properly the fulfilment of a relation—a relation between the soul and Jesus Christ; to have our hearts linked with Him, as the branches with the vine; to have His Spirit established within us as the supreme and controlling force. The Christian life is not, in itself, doing anything or believing anything; it is, at root, simply the submission of the self to the influence of Jesus, to have Him as the spring of all thought and feeling, speech and action, to have the soul penetrated with the spirit and influence of the Christ.

There are two rival theories which claim to lay down the conditions and explain the fact of discipleship. The one says that we are saved by doing certain things, by fulfilling certain outward obligations; that is called Salvation by Works. The other declares that we are saved by believing certain doctrines —that is often miscalled Salvation by Faith, it should be described as Salvation by Belief.

Neither of these theories is satisfactory.

The real doctrine of Salvation by Faith is just this, that we are saved by the absolute submission of the self to the influence of Jesus.

The Roman Church is the great advocate of the theory of Salvation by Works. "The Christian Life," it says, "is the fulfilment of certain external obligations laid upon the disciple by the Church."

In some of the later forms of Protestantism we have been taught the theory of Salvation by Belief, that the Christian Life is the acceptance of certain doctrines, which, it is claimed, embody the teachings of the New Testament.

Distinguished from both of these there is the doctrine of Salvation by Faith; the great principle for which the first reformers stood, out of which Protestantism grew, by which the absolute power of the Roman Church was broken, and to which Protestantism is nowadays returning—that the Christian Life consists neither in doing certain acts nor in believing certain doctrines, but just in the acceptance of the control and mastership of Jesus, yielding the heart to Him and allowing ourselves to be dominated by Him. It is obedience in the higher sense, not the obedience of the slave, but obedience which is the sympathetic response to an overmastering spiritual passion.

It is hardly necessary to point out that, when Jesus Christ thus dominates us, when our consciousness is penetrated by His, when He has kindled within us the spark of the new and divine life, then all our conduct, all the external side of life will be Christianized, and in our beliefs we shall, by the spirit of Jesus, be led to right doctrines and into an adequate perception of Truth, since "Truth is in Jesus."

The Christian Life is the fulfilment of a relation generating a new spiritual force which works from within outward, until the uttermost reaches of life are penetrated and energized. To put it the reverse way is to mistake the effect for the cause, the cause for the effect.

Adapting an old proverb we can say: Take care that Jesus Christ rules and controls the inner life of the soul, and the external life of conduct and belief will take care of itself.

If our hearts are under the spell of Christ, if we yield ourselves to Him in love, then our conduct will follow true lines; we shall act nobly, and think truly; the outward life will be stamped with the character of the Christ, and our beliefs, however much they may vary in form, will be the expression of a real perception of Truth.

And this view of the Christian Life solves a great and practical difficulty which meets the earnest disciple.

The worthy passion of all manhood deserving the name, is to live a good and noble life; to act purely, to be pure and holy in thought and word and deed, to carry on life's activities on a high level, to rise in conduct above all that is mean and low, vulgar and sinful. "Ah!" it is said, "to live that way is to live the Christian Life. But that is just our difficulty. It is all very well to point us to this high ideal and tell us to achieve it. We want to know how it is to be done. We try and fail often enough. We need some sufficient impulse." If Jesus points us to the ideal, and then has nothing more that He can do, we are of all men most miserable, and He is not of much more use to us than, say, Buddha, who pointed us fairly high. The whole difficulty is this, how are we to attain, to reach the higher peaks of manhood? St. Paul expressed the practical difficulty as he found it in his own experience, when he said, "The good which I would, I do not; but the evil which I would not that do I practise."

The manhood in him cried out for help, for enfranchisement from the slavery of spiritual incompetence. How is he to do the good which he would, and not the evil which he would not? He has found the secret, when, likewise out of his own individual experience, he exclaims, "I thank God through Jesus Christ our Lord."

"Link yourself with Jesus," he seems to say, "and He will give you the needful impulse." That noble life which is the dream and desire of all true men is attained in possibility, and gradually realizes itself, in proportion as we become possessed by Jesus Christ. That is the whole secret of Christianity.

If we have been aiming and straining to achieve the perfection of the outward life, like the great apostle who had with giant strength given himself to the enterprise, and also, like him, find ourselves drifting into disappointment and despair, let us leave it all, and try to unite ourselves in sympathy and spirit with Jesus, let Him rule in our hearts and minds, and we shall find as myriads before us have found that the great quest begins to find its splendid realization in that act of submission and union.

It is objected, perhaps, that all this is

very different from what has been generally taught. What about the standard of attainment which the Church expects us to reach before she will recognize us as "Christian," and admit us to her fellowship; what about all the doctrines and creeds which she makes the touchstone of Truth, and which she expects us to accept ere she will give us her blessing as dutiful sons?

Let them be! If you like, for the present, sweep them all on one side. We have nothing to fear. The thunder of excommunication is quite harmless. The Church can excommunicate us from her fold; she has in the past excommunicated many a noble soul of surpassing saintliness, but, thank God, neither she nor any other power can excommunicate us from Christ, or separate us from His love. Let us be content to trust Christ rather than the Church, if and whenever they seem to be in conflict.

And what does Jesus Christ say? What does He hold up as constituting the Christian life of discipleship? It is not sufficiently realized that He never demanded the acceptance of any doctrine or the participation in any rite as essential to discipleship. If any one is inclined to question that statement we can challenge him to search and find us the doctrine or the rite which Jesus made necessary to participation in His saving grace and power. He does not say: "Believe in the doctrine of My Deity." He simply says: "Believe on Me." "I am the Way, the Truth, and the Life," He cries, "try Me, and see if I will not lead you to God, and show you Truth, and give you Life." "The Father is in Me," He says, not in the way of laying down a theological dogma, but only to draw men to Him, so that they may share with Him in the Father's life.

If we have been stumbling about in the half light of doubt, amidst the impedimenta of creeds and dogmas, of rites and ceremonies and ecclesiastical organizations, it will come to us with the happy sense of a revelation that the one and sole demand of Jesus is that we should live our life with Him, and then all will follow. The whole Gospel is summed up in His own great cry which goes echoing down the ages like the music of God, "Come unto Me, all ye that labour and are heavy laden, and I will give you rest. Take My yoke upon you, and learn of Me: for I am meek and lowly in heart; and ye shall find rest unto your souls."

Butler & Tanner, The Selwood Printing Works, Frome, and London.